10-MINUTE
BRAIN GAMES
VISUAL
THINKING

About the Author

Dr. Gareth Moore is the internationally best-selling author of a wide range of brain-training and puzzle books, including *Brain Coach Intense* and Imagine's 10-Minute Brain Games series. His books have sold over a million copies and have been published in thirty different languages. He is also the creator of the online brain-training site BrainedUp.com and runs the daily puzzle site PuzzleMix.com.

10-MINUTE
BRAIN GAMES

VISUAL
THINKING

Dr. Gareth Moore

imagine!

2023 First US edition
All rights reserved, including the right of reproduction in whole or in part in any form. Charlesbridge and colophon
are registered trademarks of Charlesbridge Publishing, Inc.

At the time of publication, all URLs printed in this book were accurate and active. Charlesbridge and the author are not responsible for the content or accessibility of any website.

An Imagine Book
Published by Charlesbridge
9 Galen Street
Watertown, MA 02472
(617) 926-0329
www.imaginebooks.net

First published in Great Britain in 2021 by
Michael O'Mara Books Limited
9 Lion Yard
Tremadoc Road
London SW4 7NQ
Copyright © Michael O'Mara Books Limited 2021
Puzzles and solutions copyright © Gareth Moore 2021
Includes images from Shutterstock.com

ISBN 978-1-62354-551-2

Designed and typeset by Gareth Moore and Nicole Turner

Printed in China
10 9 8 7 6 5 4 3 2 1

▪ Introduction ▪

Welcome to *10-Minute Brain Games: Visual Thinking*, packed full of over thirty different types of challenges, with a huge range of more than three hundred puzzles to confuse and delight you in equal measure.

Ranging from nonverbal reasoning to coloring puzzles that reveal a hidden picture when solved, there's something here for everyone. Whether you want to build your visualization skills, test your abilities, or simply have some relaxing fun, you'll find something suited to you. For the best mental benefit, however, you should be sure to try all of the different types of puzzle—even those that seem the trickiest, since these are likely to be the ones that will be most beneficial for your brain.

Each puzzle is designed to be solvable in ten minutes or so, but some may go faster and others may take a bit longer. There's a handy area on each page for keeping track of your solving time.

All of the puzzles are observation-based, but what you do with those observations varies from challenge to challenge. In some cases, you merely need to spot relevant details, whereas in others you will need to make logical deductions based on those observations. For all of the latter type of puzzle, full written explanations are provided in the solution section at the back of the book, so you should never be left wondering why an answer is deemed correct! Solutions are also given for all other puzzles, too.

Have fun!

▪ Shape-Counting ▪

Instructions

How many squares and/or rectangles can you count in this image? Many of them will overlap, including the large rectangle on the outside.

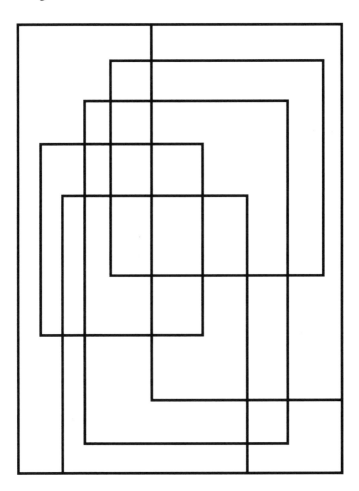

Your solving time: _____   7

▪ Pairing Problem ▪

Instructions
Join these balloons into identical pairs, allowing for rotation.

A   B   C

D   E   F

Your solving time: _____

▪ Cubic Conundrum ▪

Instructions

How many cubes are there in the following image? It began as a 5×4×4 block before some cubes were removed. None of the cubes are "floating" in midair.

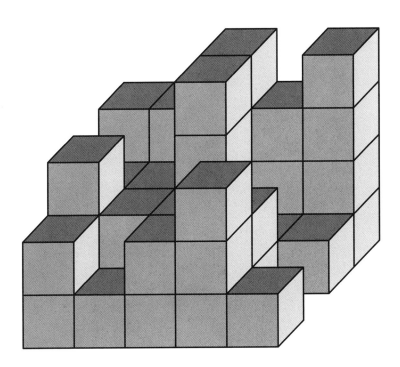

▪ Color by Pixel ▪

Instructions

Color each square according to the key to reveal a hidden picture.

1	1	1	1	2	2	2	2	2	2	2	2	2	2	2	2	1	1	1	1	
1	1	1	2	3	3	3	3	3	3	3	3	3	3	3	3	2	1	1	1	
1	1	2	3	3	3	4	3	3	3	3	3	3	4	3	3	3	3	2	1	1
1	2	5	5	5	5	5	5	5	5	5	5	5	5	4	5	5	5	2	1	
2	3	5	5	4	5	5	5	5	4	5	5	5	5	5	5	5	5	3	2	
2	5	4	3	3	3	3	3	3	3	3	3	4	3	3	3	3	3	5	2	
2	5	5	5	5	5	4	5	5	5	5	5	5	5	5	4	5	5	5	2	
1	2	2	2	2	2	2	2	2	2	2	2	2	2	2	2	2	2	2	1	
6	6	6	6	6	6	6	6	7	7	7	7	6	6	6	6	6	6	6	6	
1	8	8	8	8	8	4	4	4	4	8	8	4	4	4	8	5	8	8	1	
5	5	8	5	5	4	5	8	8	4	4	4	8	8	5	5	8	5	8	8	
7	8	8	8	8	8	8	8	8	8	8	8	8	8	8	8	8	8	8	7	
1	7	9	9	7	9	7	4	5	5	5	5	4	7	7	9	7	7	9	7	
9	7	5	5	5	7	7	9	7	9	7	7	9	7	9	5	5	9	7	9	
7	7	2	2	2	2	2	2	2	2	2	2	2	2	2	2	2	2	1	7	
1	2	5	5	5	5	5	5	5	5	5	5	5	5	5	5	5	5	2	1	
2	3	3	3	3	3	3	3	3	3	3	3	3	3	3	3	3	3	3	2	
2	3	3	5	5	5	5	5	5	5	5	5	5	5	5	5	5	3	3	2	
1	2	3	3	3	3	3	3	3	3	3	3	3	3	3	3	3	3	2	1	
1	1	2	2	2	2	2	2	2	2	2	2	2	2	2	2	2	2	1	1	

1 – light blue

2 – black

3 – orange

4 – yellow

5 – light orange

6 – red

7 – green

8 – brown

9 – light green

Your solving time: _____

▪ Shipshape ▪

Instructions

Which of the images, A to F, exactly matches a portion of the main image?

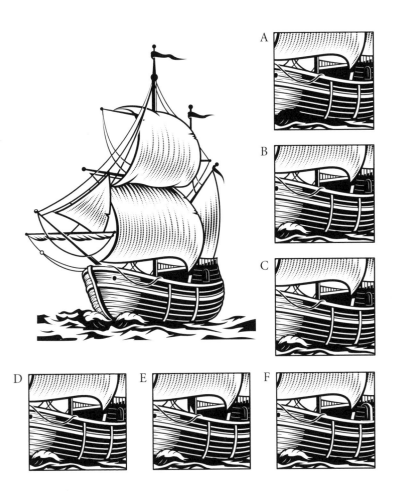

▪ Fold and Punch ▪

Instructions
Imagine folding and then punching paper as shown. Unfold, and which image results?

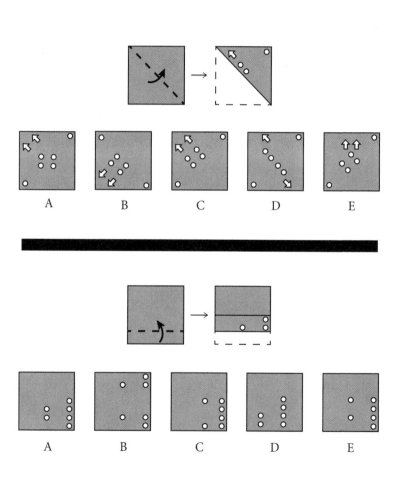

Your solving time: _____

▪ Crack the Code ▪

Instructions

Crack the code used to describe each image and circle the correct identifier for the image on the second line of each puzzle.

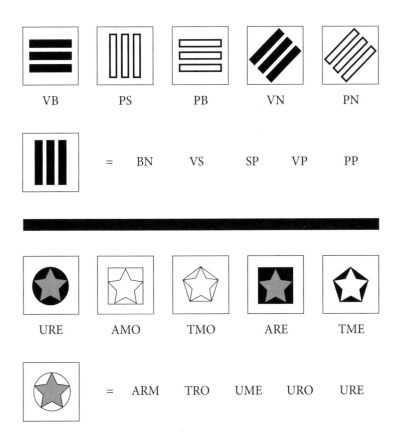

VB   PS   PB   VN   PN

=   BN   VS   SP   VP   PP

URE   AMO   TMO   ARE   TME

=   ARM   TRO   UME   URO   URE

▪ **Mirror Image** ▪

Instructions

Which of the options, A to D, is an exact mirror image of the jet?

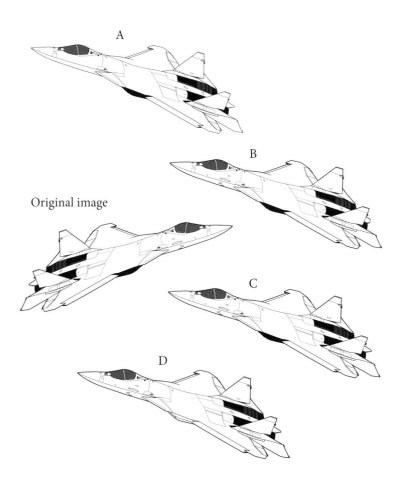

A

B

Original image

C

D

Your solving time: _____

▪ Dot to Dot ▪

Instructions

Join the dots with straight lines in increasing numerical order, starting at "1" (marked with a star), to reveal a hidden picture.

■ **Pattern Poser** ■

Instructions

Which of the options, A to E, should be placed into the empty box in order to complete the pattern?

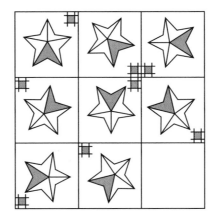

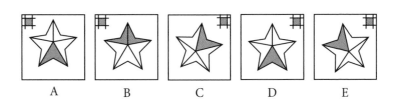

Your solving time: _____

▪ Odd One Out ▪

Instructions
Which image is the odd one out on each line?

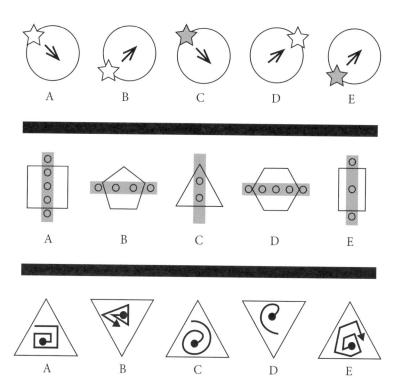

▪ Shape Nets ▪

Instructions

Which of the patterns, A to D, could be cut out and folded to match the view shown at the top?

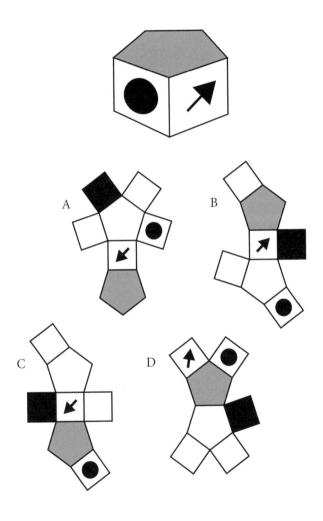

Your solving time: _____

▪ Cake Cut ▪

Instructions

Which of the images, A to F, exactly matches a portion of the main image?

■ Fold and Punch ■

Instructions
Imagine folding and then punching paper as shown. Unfold, and which image results?

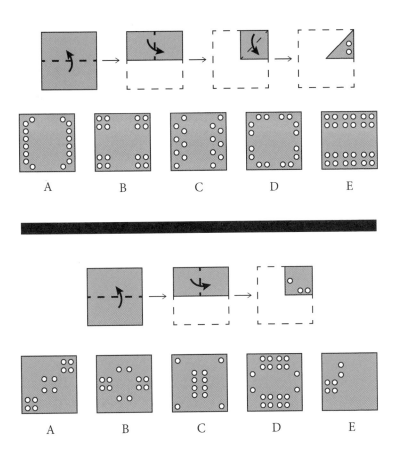

Your solving time: _____

▪ Rectangle Maze ▪

Instructions
Find your way through the maze.

▪ **Sequences** ▪

Instructions

Which option, from A to E, should replace the question-mark symbols in order to continue each sequence?

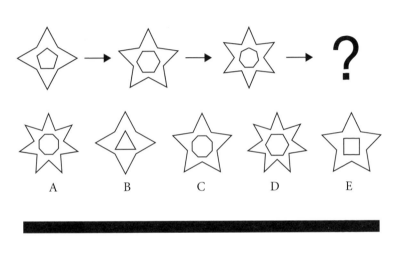

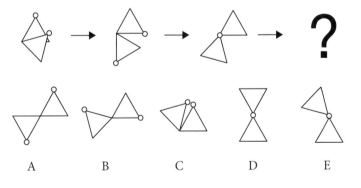

Your solving time: _____

▪ Incorrect Cube ▪

Instructions

If you were to cut out and fold this image to make a six-sided cube, which of the cube images beneath, A to E, could not be formed?

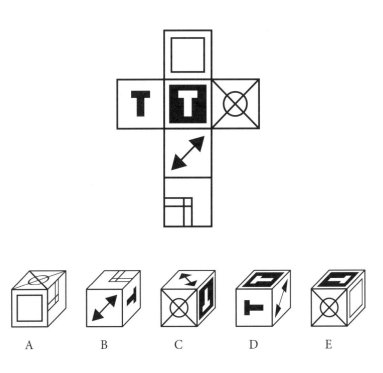

| A | B | C | D | E |

▪ Matching Halves ▪

Instructions

Join the eight halves together to make four complete cars.

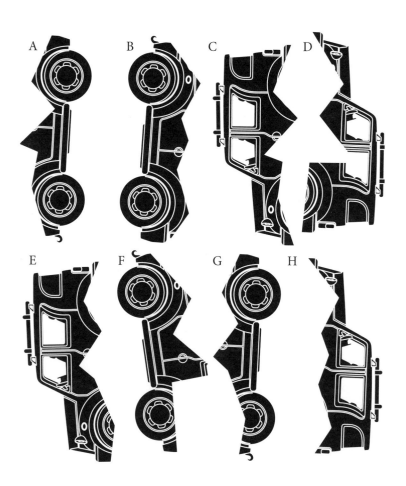

Your solving time: _____

▪ Steamed Out ▪

Instructions

Which of the images, A to F, exactly matches a portion of the main image?

Your solving time: _____   25

▪ Fold and Punch ▪

Instructions

Imagine folding and then punching paper as shown. Unfold, and which image results?

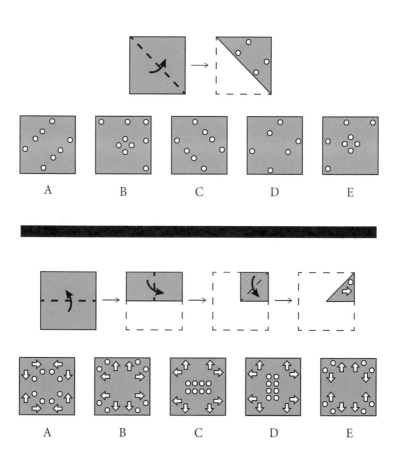

Your solving time: _____

▪ Shape-Counting ▪

Instructions

How many squares and/or rectangles can you count in this image? Many of them will overlap, including the large rectangle on the outside.

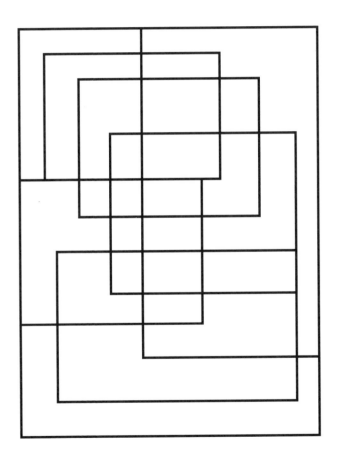

Your solving time: _____

■ **Pairing Problem** ■

Instructions

Join these cakes into identical pairs, allowing for rotation.

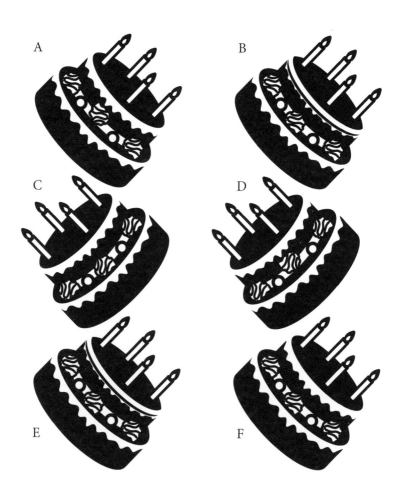

Your solving time: _____

■ Dot to Dot ■

Instructions

Join the dots with straight lines in increasing numerical order, starting at "1" (marked with a star), to reveal a hidden picture.

Your solving time: _____   **29**

▪ **Pattern Poser** ▪

Instructions

Which of the options, A to E, should be placed into the empty box in order to complete the pattern?

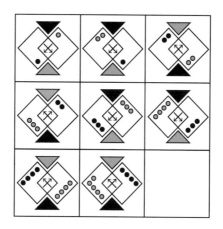

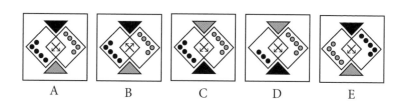

Your solving time: _____

▪ Odd One Out ▪

Instructions
Which image is the odd one out on each line?

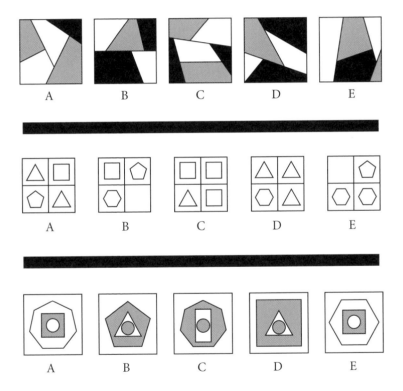

▪ Shape Nets ▪

Instructions

Which of the patterns, A to D, could be cut out and folded to match the view shown at the top?

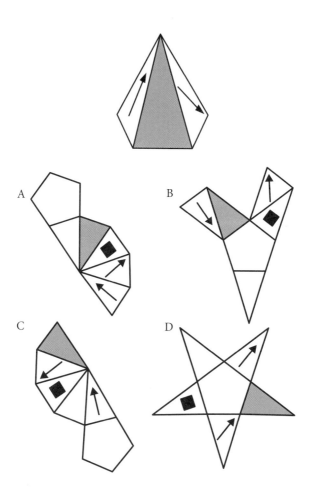

Your solving time: _____

▪ Crack the Code ▪

Instructions

Crack the code used to describe each image and circle the correct identifier for the image on the second line of each puzzle.

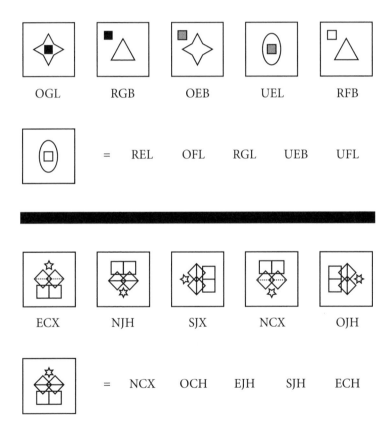

▪ **Mirror Image** ▪

Instructions
Which of the options, A to E, is an exact mirror image of the giraffe?

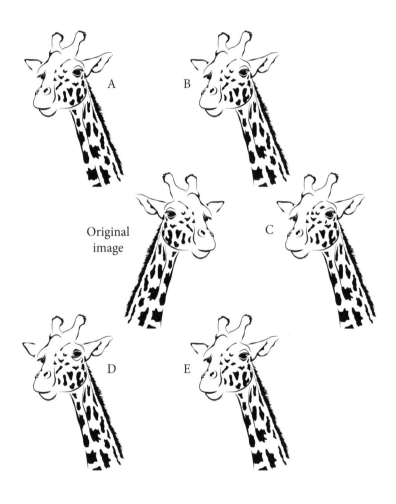

Your solving time: _____

▪ Spot the Cube ▪

Instructions

If you were to cut out and fold this image to make a six-sided cube, which of the cube images beneath, A to E, is the only one that could be formed?

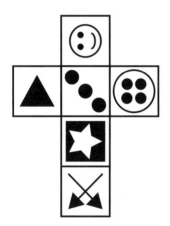

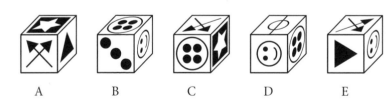

  A   B   C   D   E

Your solving time: _____

▪ Find the Pair ▪

Instructions

Which two of these backpacks are identical, allowing for rotation?

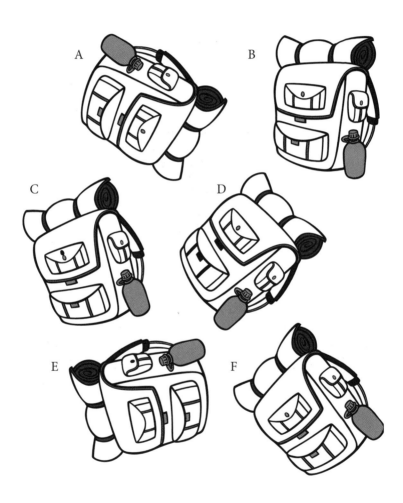

Your solving time: _____

▪ Hidden Image ▪

Instructions

Which of the options, A to D, conceals the image shown on the far left of each row? It may be rotated, but all elements of it must be visible.

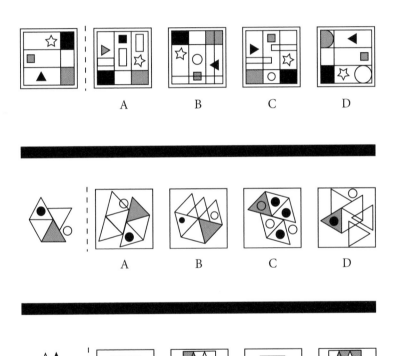

Your solving time: _____   37

▪ Top View ▪

Instructions

Which of the options, A to E, represents the view of the
3D object when seen from the direction of the arrow?

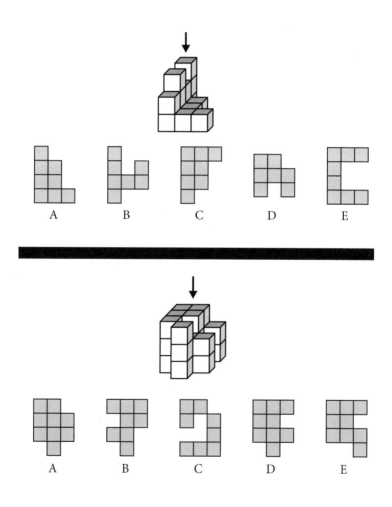

Your solving time: _____

▪ **Cubic Conundrum** ▪

Instructions

How many cubes are there in the following image? It began as a 5×4×4 block before some cubes were removed. None of the cubes are "floating" in midair.

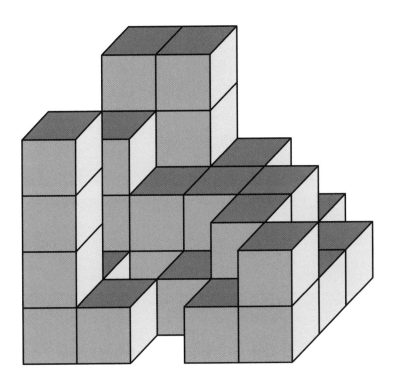

Your solving time: _____

▪ Color by Pixel ▪

Instructions

Color each square according to the key to reveal a hidden picture.

1	1	2	2	2	1	1	3	3	3	3	3	3	1	1	2	2	2	1	1
1	2	2	1	1	3	3	4	4	4	4	3	5	3	3	1	1	2	2	1
2	2	1	3	3	6	6	7	6	6	6	3	5	5	5	3	3	1	2	2
2	1	3	5	8	3	6	7	7	7	6	7	3	3	5	3	4	3	1	2
2	1	3	5	5	3	3	6	7	7	7	6	7	7	3	4	4	3	3	2
2	3	5	5	5	8	3	6	6	7	7	7	6	7	7	7	3	8	3	1
1	3	5	5	5	5	8	3	3	6	7	7	7	6	7	3	9	8	3	1
3	4	3	9	9	5	8	8	8	3	7	7	7	6	7	3	9	8	8	3
3	4	4	3	9	8	8	8	8	3	6	7	6	7	7	3	9	9	8	3
3	7	6	3	9	9	9	3	3	6	7	7	6	7	7	3	9	9	5	3
3	6	7	6	3	3	9	3	6	7	7	7	7	6	7	7	3	3	3	3
3	6	7	7	6	6	3	8	3	7	7	7	7	7	6	7	7	6	4	3
3	4	6	7	7	7	6	3	6	6	3	3	3	7	7	6	6	6	4	3
1	3	4	6	7	7	6	6	7	3	5	5	8	3	7	7	7	4	3	1
1	3	4	6	6	7	7	7	7	3	5	5	8	3	7	7	7	4	3	1
1	1	3	7	7	6	7	7	7	6	3	9	5	8	3	4	4	3	1	2
2	1	3	4	4	7	6	6	6	7	7	3	9	8	8	3	4	3	1	2
2	1	1	3	3	4	4	7	7	7	4	3	9	8	3	3	3	1	2	2
1	2	1	1	1	3	3	4	4	4	3	9	9	3	3	1	1	2	2	1
1	1	2	2	1	1	1	3	3	3	3	3	3	1	1	2	2	2	1	1

1 – light gray   5 – dark green   9 – yellow
2 – gray   6 – light blue
3 – black   7 – blue
4 – dark blue   8 – green

Your solving time: _____

▪ Tracing Paper ▪

Instructions

Which of the options, A to E, represents the view of the image shown at the top when folded in half along the dashed line? Assume it has been drawn on transparent paper.

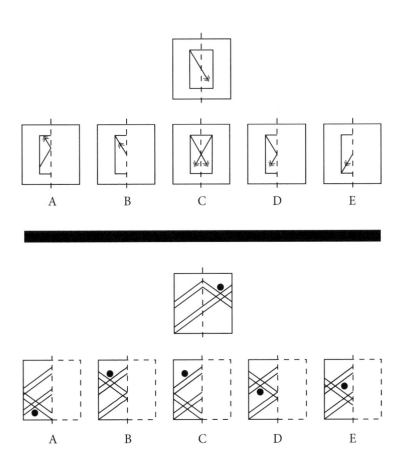

▪ A New View ▪

Instructions

Which of the options, A to D, represents a view of the first 3D object when seen from the direction of the arrow?

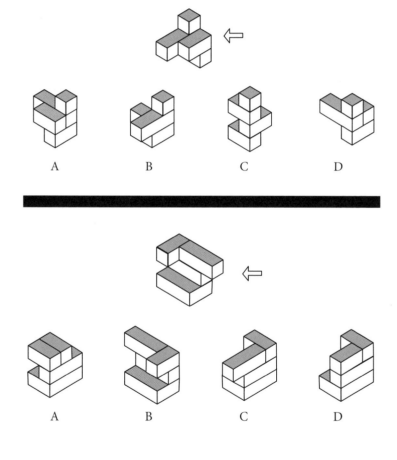

Your solving time: _____

▪ Upon Reflection ▪

Instructions

Which of the options, A to E, would result when each image is reflected in the dashed line shown?

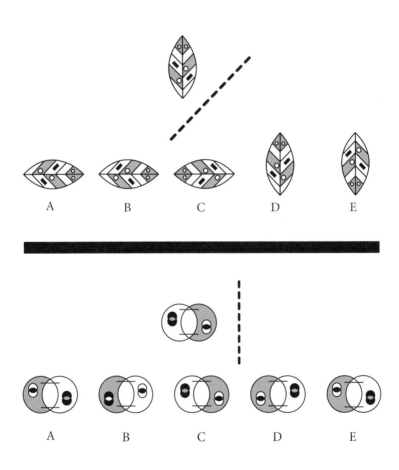

▪ **Color by Shape** ▪

Instructions

Color each shape according to the key to reveal a hidden picture.

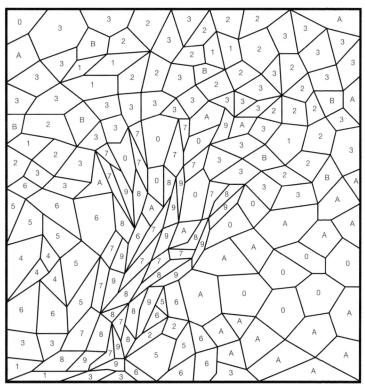

1 – light green	5 – gray	9 – dark brown
2 – green	6 – dark gray	0 – white
3 – dark green	7 – light brown	A – orange
4 – light gray	8 – brown	B – red

Your solving time: _____

▪ **Building Blocks** ▪

Instructions

Which of the sets of blocks, A to D, can be rearranged to form the assembly shown? All blocks must be used exactly once each.

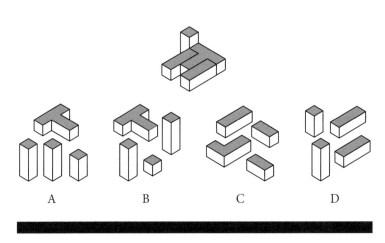

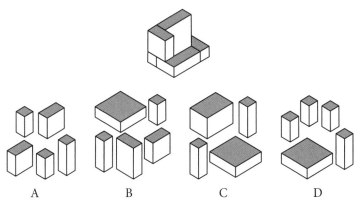

▪ Missing Face ▪

Instructions

Which of the options, A to E, should replace the blank face on the cube so that they all become different views of the same cube? The correct face may need rotating.

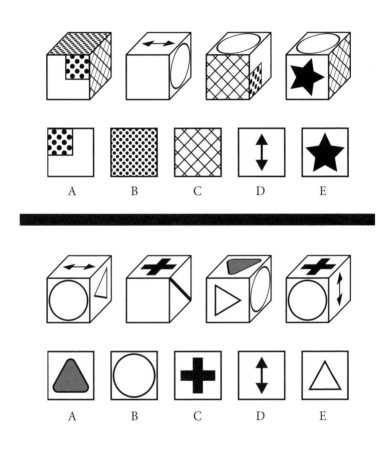

Your solving time: _____

▪ Elephant Enigma ▪

Instructions

Which of the images, A to F, exactly matches a portion of the main image?

Your solving time: _____   47

▪ Fold and Punch ▪

Instructions

Imagine folding and then punching paper as shown. Unfold, and which image results?

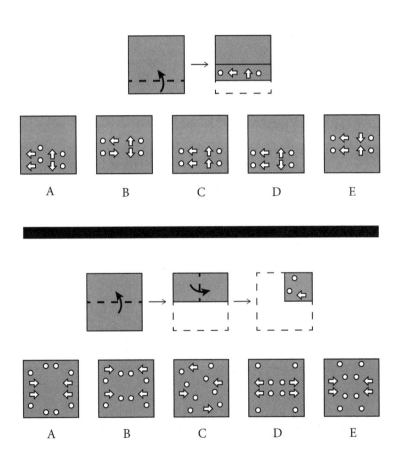

▪ Hidden Image ▪

Instructions

Which of the options, A to D, conceals the image shown on the far left of each row? It may be rotated, but all elements of it must be visible.

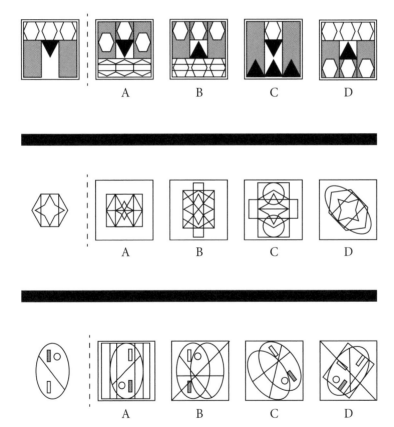

▪ Side View ▪

Instructions
Which of the options, A to E, represents the view of the 3D object when seen from the direction of the arrow?

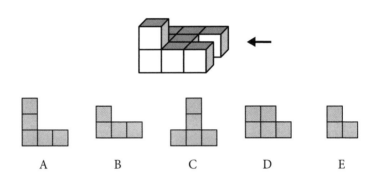

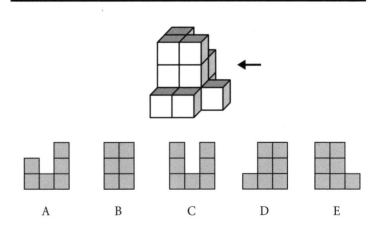

Your solving time: _____

▪ Find the Rule ▪

Instructions

Based on the given example transformations, which of the options from A to E should replace the question-mark symbol?

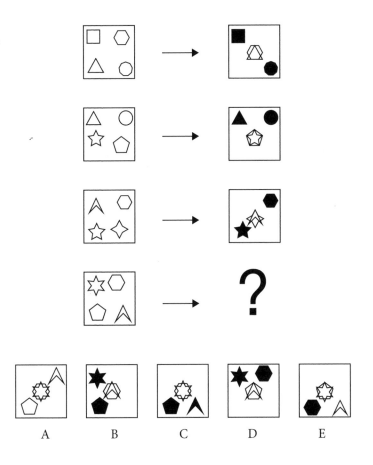

A   B   C   D   E

▪ Spot the Changes ▪

Instructions
Can you find the five differences between the two images?

Your solving time: _____

▪ Building Blocks ▪

Instructions

Which of the sets of blocks, A to D, can be rearranged to form the assembly shown? All blocks must be used exactly once each.

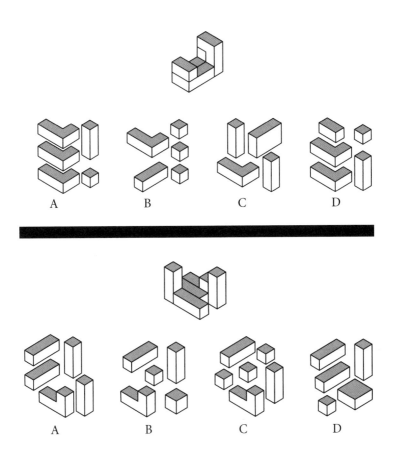

▪ Missing Face ▪

Instructions

Which of the options, A to E, should replace the blank face on the cube so that they all become different views of the same cube? The correct face may need rotating.

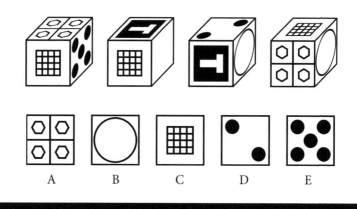

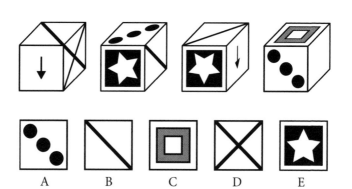

Your solving time: _____

▪ Hidden Image ▪

Instructions

Which of the options, A to D, conceals the image shown on the far left of each row? It may be rotated, but all elements of it must be visible.

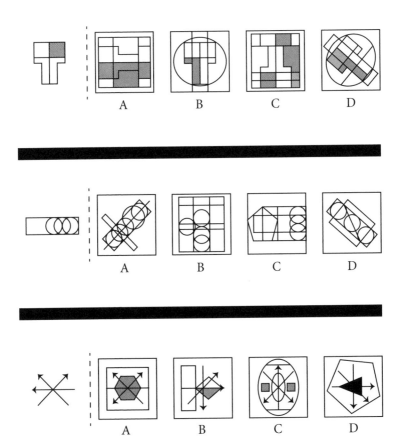

▪ Side and Top View ▪

Instructions

Which of the options, A to E, represents the view of the 3D object when seen from the direction of the arrow?

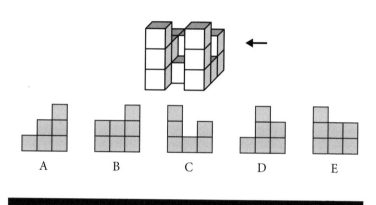

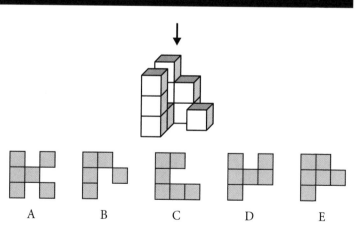

Your solving time: _____

▪ Upon Reflection ▪

Instructions

Which of the options, A to E, would result when each image is reflected in the dashed line shown?

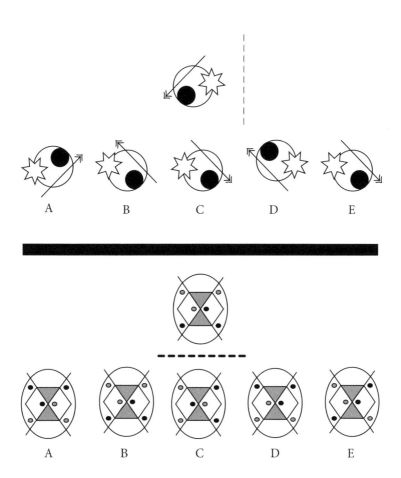

A   B   C   D   E

A   B   C   D   E

▪ **Color by Shape** ▪

Instructions

Color each shape according to the key to reveal a hidden picture.

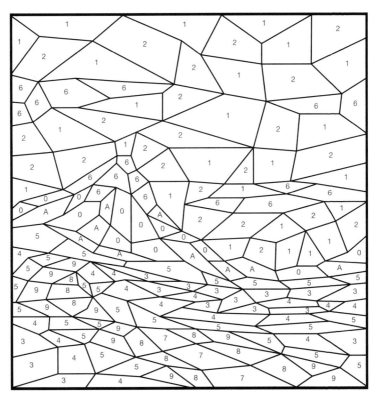

1 – light blue	5 – dark green	9 – dark brown
2 – blue	6 – white	0 – light gray
3 – light green	7 – light brown	A – gray
4 – green	8 – brown	

Your solving time: _____

▪ Shape-Counting ▪

Instructions

How many squares and/or rectangles can you count in this image? Many of them will overlap.

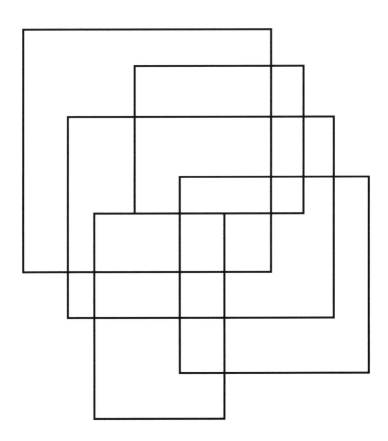

▪ Pairing Problem ▪

Instructions
Join these DJs into identical pairs, allowing for rotation.

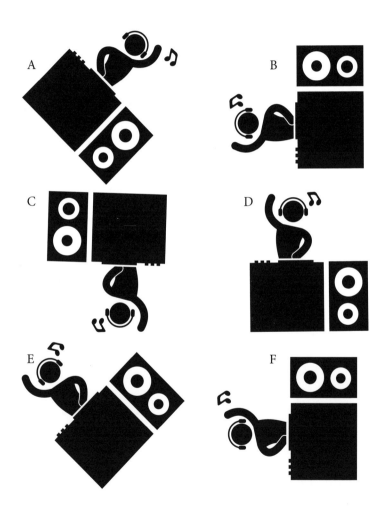

Your solving time: _____

▪ Spot the Cube ▪

Instructions

If you were to cut out and fold this image to make a six-sided cube, which of the cube images beneath, A to E, is the only one that could be formed?

A   B   C   D   E

▪ **Find the Pair** ▪

Instructions

Which two of these images are identical, allowing for rotation?

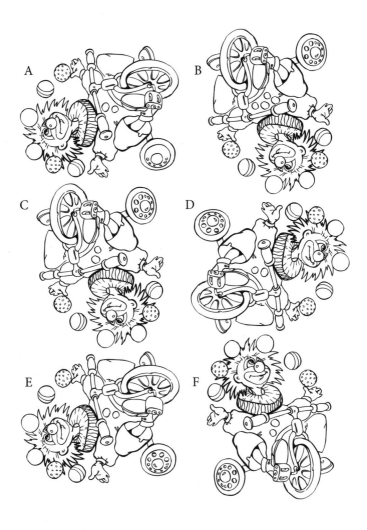

Your solving time: _____

▪ **Dot to Dot** ▪

Instructions

Join the dots with straight lines in increasing numerical order, starting at "1" (marked with a star), to reveal a hidden picture.

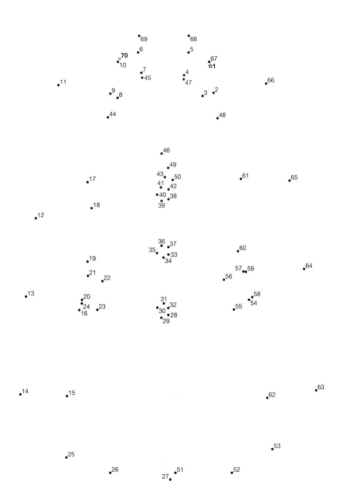

Your solving time: _____   **63**

▪ **Pattern Poser** ▪

Instructions

Which of the options, A to E, should be placed into the empty box in order to complete the pattern?

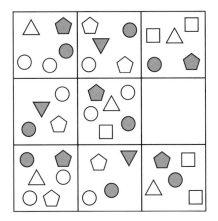

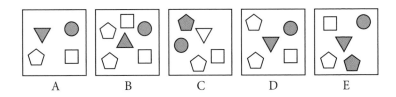

Your solving time: _____

▪ Find the Rule ▪

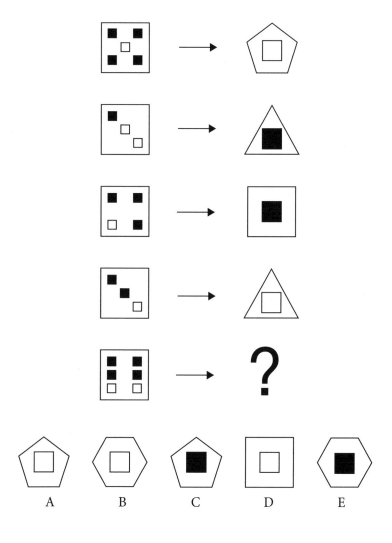

▪ Spot the Changes ▪

Instructions
Can you find the five differences between the two images?

Your solving time: _____

▪ Incorrect Cube ▪

Instructions

If you were to cut out and fold this image to make a six-sided cube, which of the cube images beneath, A to E, could not be formed?

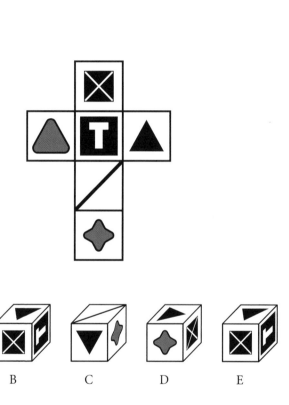

A   B   C   D   E

▪ Matching Halves ▪

Instructions
Join the eight halves together to make four complete strawberries.

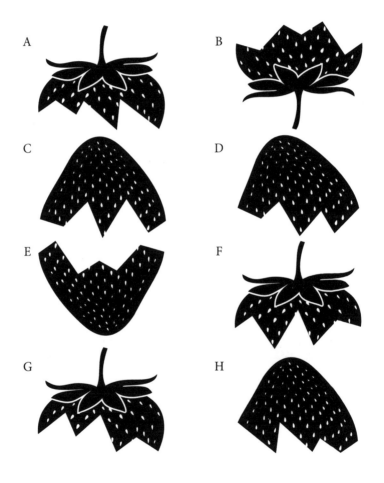

Your solving time: _____

▪ Rectangle Maze ▪

Instructions
Find your way through the maze.

▪ Sequences ▪

Instructions

Which option, from A to E, should replace the question-mark symbols in order to continue each sequence?

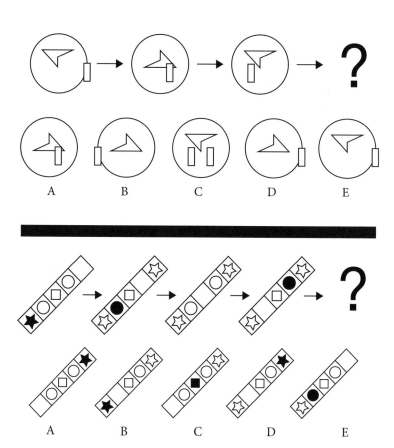

Your solving time: _____

■ Floral Focus ■

Instructions
Which of the images, A to F, exactly matches a portion of the main image?

▪ Transform Again ▪

Instructions

Which option, from A to E, should replace the question-mark symbol? The rule applied on the left of the ":" should also be applied on the right.

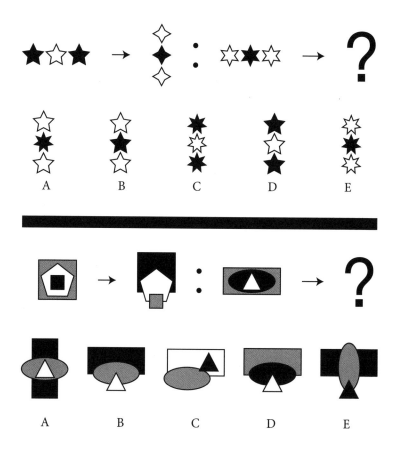

Your solving time: _____

▪ Dot to Dot ▪

Instructions

Join the dots with straight lines in increasing numerical order, starting at "1" (marked with a star), to reveal a hidden picture.

Your solving time: _____

▪ **Pattern Poser** ▪

Instructions

Which of the options, A to E, should be placed into the empty box in order to complete the pattern?

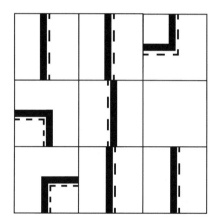

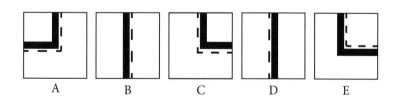

| A | B | C | D | E |

Your solving time: _____

▪ Tracing Paper ▪

Instructions

Which of the options, A to E, represents the view of the image shown at the top when folded in half along the dashed line? Assume it has been drawn on transparent paper.

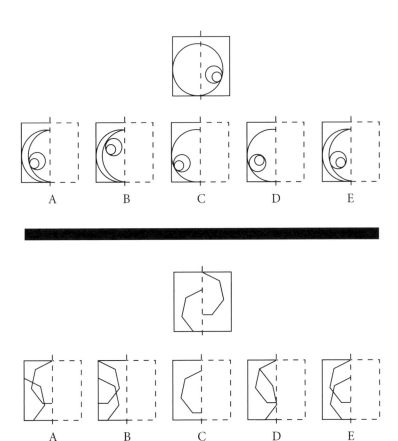

Your solving time: _____   75

▪ A New View ▪

Instructions

Which of the options, A to D, represents a view of the first 3D object when seen from the direction of the arrow?

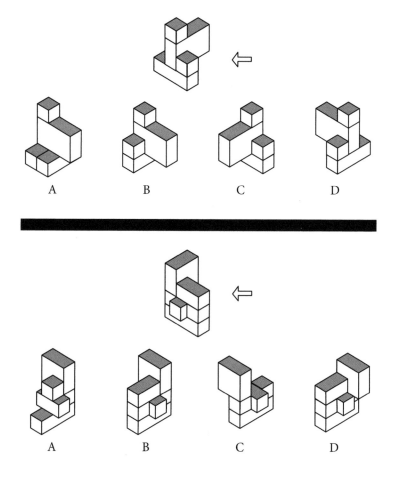

Your solving time: _____

▪ **Shape-Counting** ▪

Instructions

How many squares and/or rectangles can you count in this image? Many of them will overlap.

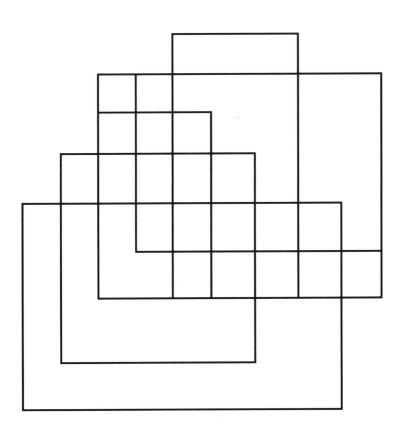

▪ **Pairing Problem** ▪

Instructions

Join these bunches of flowers into identical pairs, allowing for rotation.

Your solving time: _____

▪ **Find the Rule** ▪

Instructions

Based on the given example transformations, which of the options from A to E should replace the question-mark symbol?

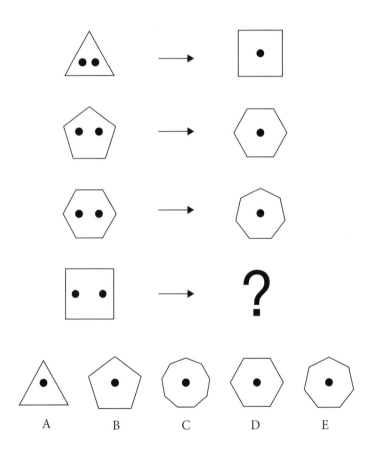

▪ Illusory Image ▪

Instructions

Use a ruler and a bold, dark marker to join the four dots to form a perfect straight-edged square. But what do you notice once this is drawn?

Your solving time: _____

▪ Cubic Conundrum ▪

Instructions

How many cubes are there in the following image? It began as a 5×5×5 block before some cubes were removed. None of the cubes are "floating" in midair.

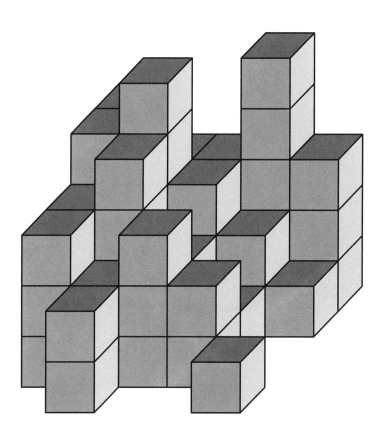

▪ Color by Pixel ▪

Instructions

Color each square according to the key to reveal a hidden picture.

```
1 1 1 1 2 3 3 3 3 1 2 2 1 1 2 1 1 2 1 1
2 1 1 2 3 4 4 4 4 3 2 3 3 3 2 2 2 2 2 1 1
1 1 2 2 3 4 5 5 4 4 3 4 4 4 3 2 2 1 1 2
1 1 3 3 4 4 4 5 4 4 4 5 5 4 3 2 2 2 1 1
1 3 4 4 4 4 3 6 6 3 6 5 5 4 3 2 2 2 1 1
2 3 4 5 5 4 6 7 7 7 6 6 4 4 3 2 2 1 1 2
1 3 4 4 5 5 6 7 6 7 3 4 4 3 2 2 2 2 1 1
1 1 3 3 4 4 3 7 7 7 6 6 4 4 3 2 2 2 1 1
1 1 2 2 3 4 6 6 6 3 6 5 5 5 4 3 2 1 1 1
1 1 2 3 4 4 5 5 4 4 4 5 5 5 4 3 2 2 1 2
2 1 1 3 4 5 5 5 4 4 3 4 4 4 4 3 2 2 1 1
1 1 2 3 4 5 5 4 4 4 3 3 3 3 3 2 2 1 1 1
1 2 2 2 3 4 4 4 3 3 3 2 2 2 8 8 9 9 9 1
1 9 9 8 2 3 3 3 0 0 2 8 8 8 9 9 9 8 8 0 1
2 1 0 9 8 8 2 2 9 0 2 8 9 9 8 8 8 0 1 2
1 1 0 0 9 9 8 8 9 0 A 9 8 8 8 8 8 0 1 1
A A B A 0 0 9 0 9 0 8 8 8 8 8 8 0 A A A
B B B A A A A A 9 0 9 0 0 0 0 0 0 0 A B B
A A B B B B B B B B B B B B B B B B B B A
A A A A B A A A A B B B A A A A A A A A A
```

1 – blue	5 – light orange	9 – light green
2 – light blue	6 – orange	0 – dark green
3 – dark red	7 – yellow	A – brown
4 – red	8 – green	B – light brown

Your solving time: _____

▪ Find the Rule ▪

Instructions

Based on the given example transformations, which of the options from A to E should replace the question-mark symbol?

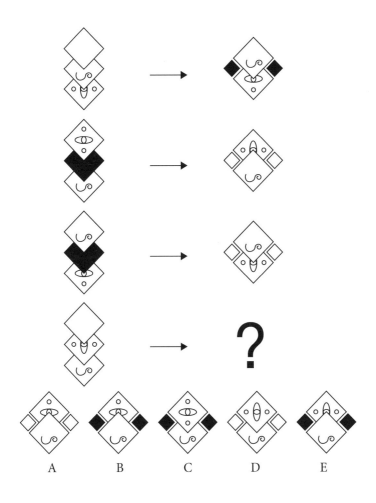

▪ Illusory Image ▪

Instructions

Which of the three horizontal rectangles do you think is identical in size to the topmost, vertical rectangle? Check if you are correct.

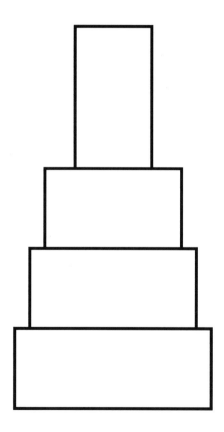

Your solving time: _____

▪ Dot to Dot ▪

Instructions

Join the dots with straight lines in increasing numerical order, starting at "1" (marked with a star), to reveal a hidden picture.

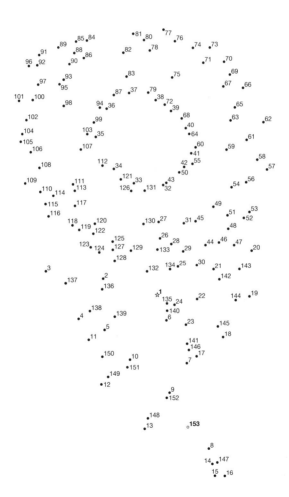

Your solving time: _____   85

▪ **Pattern Poser** ▪

Instructions

Which of the options, A to E, should be placed into the empty box in order to complete the pattern?

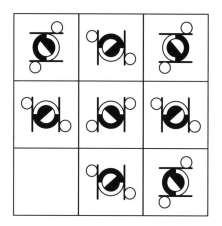

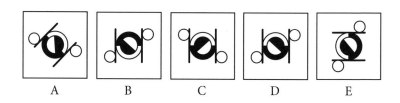

Your solving time: _____

▪ Spot the Cube ▪

Instructions

If you were to cut out and fold this image to make a six-sided cube, which of the cube images beneath, A to E, is the only one that could be formed?

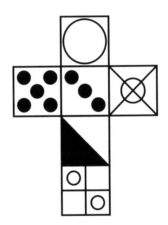

A   B   C   D   E

▪ Find the Pair ▪

Instructions

Which two of these butterflies are identical, allowing for rotation?

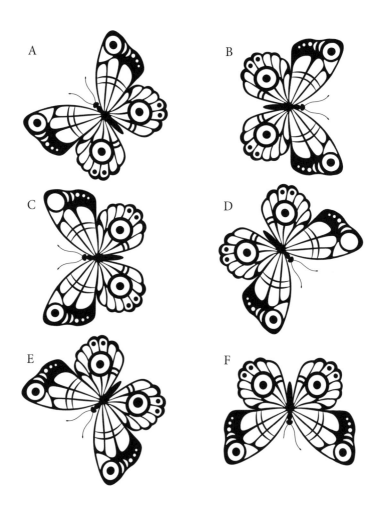

Your solving time: _____

▪ Building Blocks ▪

Instructions
Which of the sets of blocks, A to D, can be rearranged to form the assembly shown? All blocks must be used exactly once each.

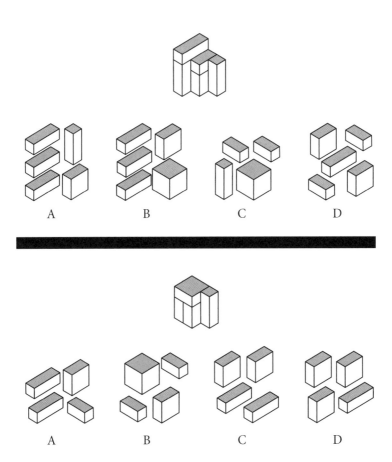

▪ Missing Face ▪

Instructions

Which of the options, A to E, should replace the blank face on the cube so that they all become different views of the same cube? The correct face may need rotating.

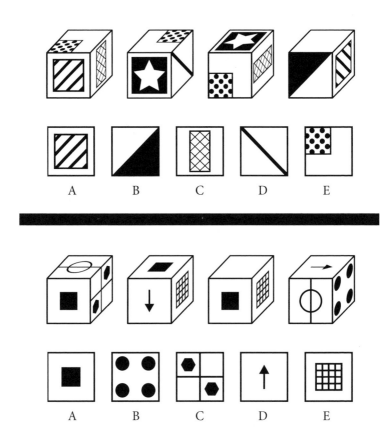

Your solving time: _____

▪ **Find the Rule** ▪

Instructions
Based on the given example transformations, which of the options from A to E should replace the question-mark symbol?

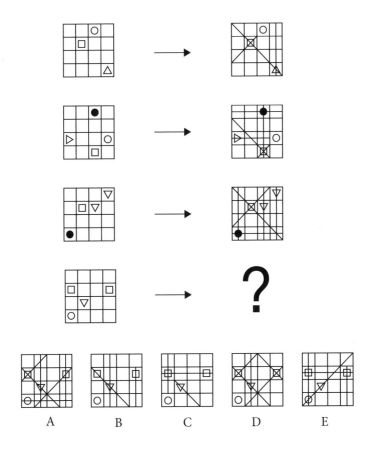

▪ Illusory Image ▪

Instructions

Color the gray squares a dark color, such as black. Now draw bold, dark lines on the unbroken diagonals. What happens to these lines?

Your solving time: _____

▪ Odd One Out ▪

Instructions
Which image is the odd one out on each line?

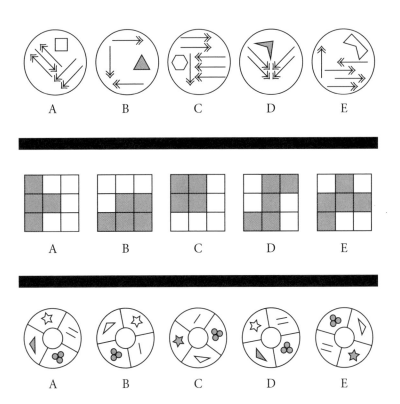

A   B   C   D   E

A   B   C   D   E

A   B   C   D   E

Your solving time: _____

▪ Shape Nets ▪

Instructions

Which of the patterns, A to D, could be cut out and folded to match the view shown at the top?

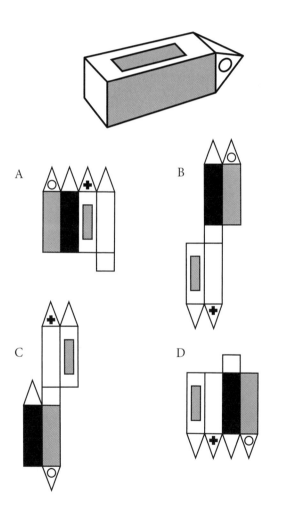

94   **Your solving time:** _____

▪ Upon Rotation ▪

Instructions

Which of the options, A to E, is exactly the same as the first image of each puzzle, apart from its scale and the angle of its rotation?

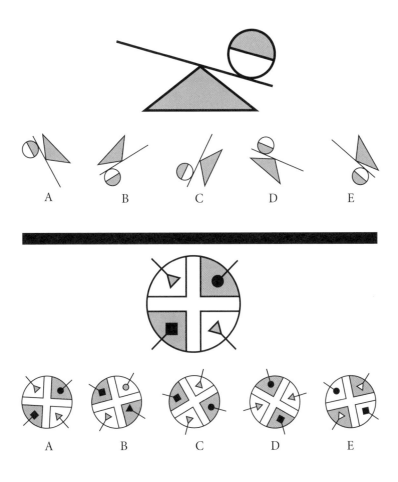

■ Color By Shape ■

Instructions

Color each shape according to the key to reveal a hidden picture.

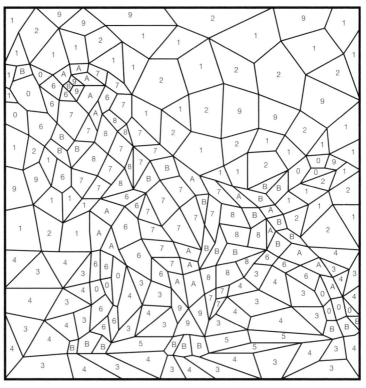

1 – pale blue	5 – dark green	9 – white
2 – light blue	6 – light brown	0 – light gray
3 – light green	7 – brown	A – gray
4 – green	8 – dark brown	B – dark gray

Your solving time: _____

▪ Hidden Image ▪

Instructions

Which of the options, A to D, conceals the image shown on the far left of each row? It may be rotated, but all elements of it must be visible.

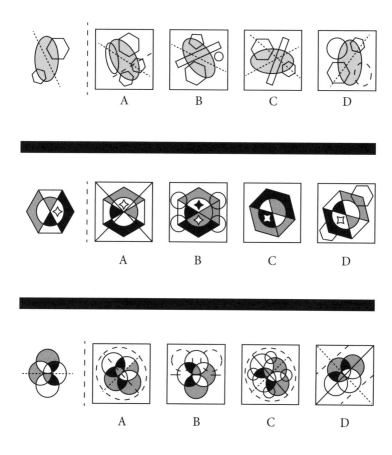

■ Top View ■

Instructions

Which of the options, A to E, represents the view of the 3D object when seen from the direction of the arrow?

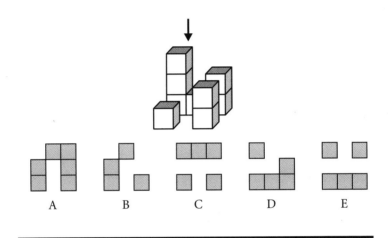

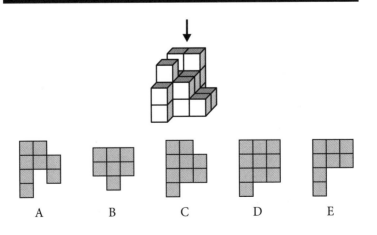

Your solving time: _____

▪ Tracing Paper ▪

Instructions

Which of the options, A to E, represents the view of the image shown at the top when folded in half along the dashed line? Assume it has been drawn on transparent paper.

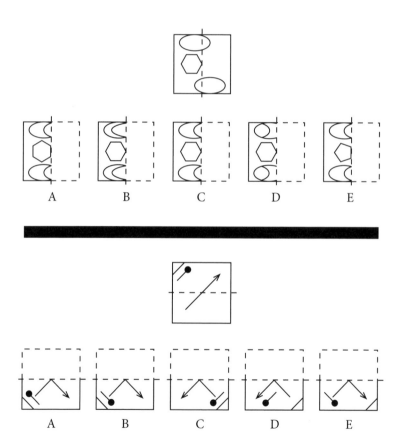

▪ A New View ▪

Instructions

Which of the options, A to D, represents a view of the first 3D object when seen from the direction of the arrow?

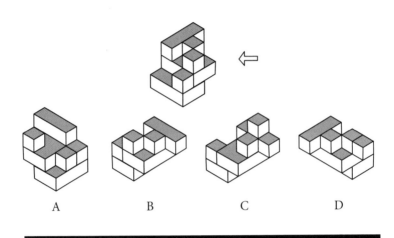

A   B   C   D

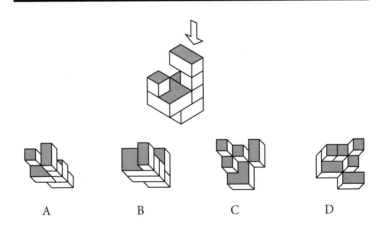

A   B   C   D

Your solving time: _____

▪ Find the Rule ▪

Instructions

Based on the given example transformations, which of the options from A to E should replace the question-mark symbol?

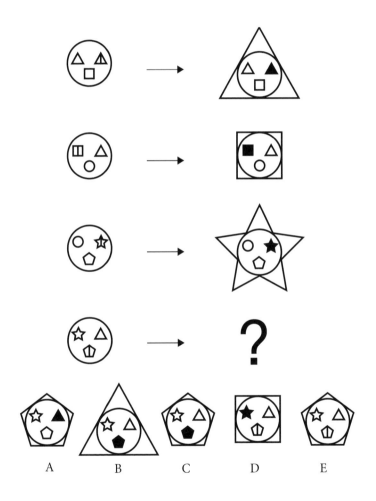

▪ Illusory Image ▪

Instructions
Compare the two central squares. Which do you think is the larger?

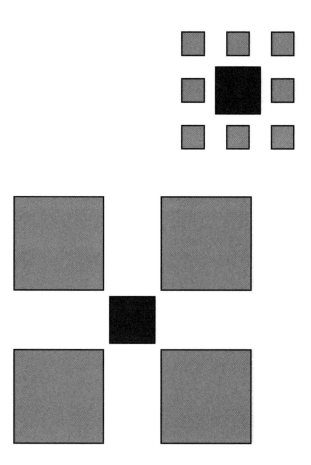

Your solving time: _____

▪ Shape-Counting ▪

Instructions

How many triangles, including those formed via overlaps, can you count in this image?

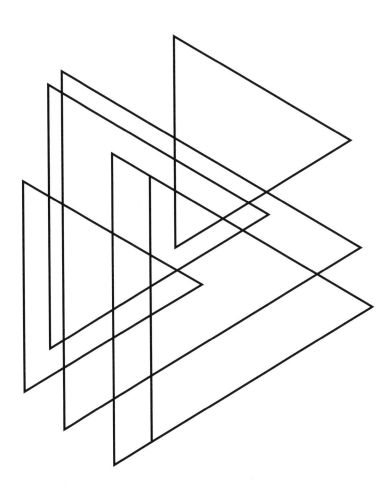

▪ Pairing Problem ▪

Instructions
Join these cooking pots into identical pairs, allowing for rotation.

Your solving time: _____

▪ Hidden Image ▪

Instructions

Which of the options, A to D, conceals the image shown on the far left of each row? It may be rotated, but all elements of it must be visible.

        A   B   C   D

        A   B   C   D

▪ Side View ▪

Instructions

Which of the options, A to E, represents the view of the 3D object when seen from the direction of the arrow?

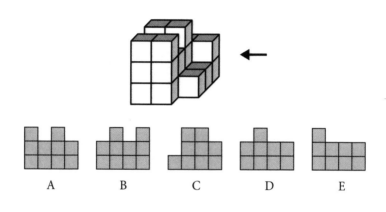

A B C D E

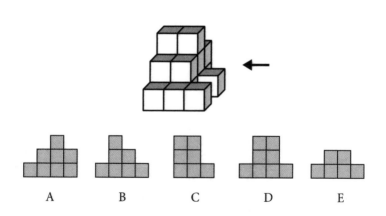

A B C D E

Your solving time: _____

▪ Dot to Dot ▪

Instructions

Join the dots with straight lines in increasing numerical order, starting at "1" (marked with a star), to reveal a hidden picture.

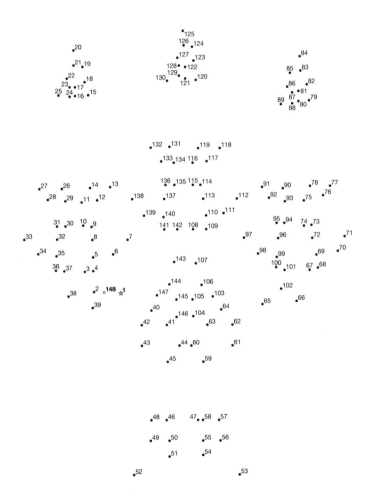

Your solving time: _____

▪ Pattern Poser ▪

Instructions

Which of the options, A to E, should be placed into the empty box in order to complete the pattern?

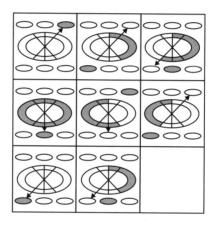

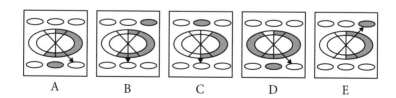

Your solving time: _____

▪ Cubic Conundrum ▪

Instructions

How many cubes are there in the following image? It began as a 5×5×5 block before some cubes were removed. None of the cubes are "floating" in midair.

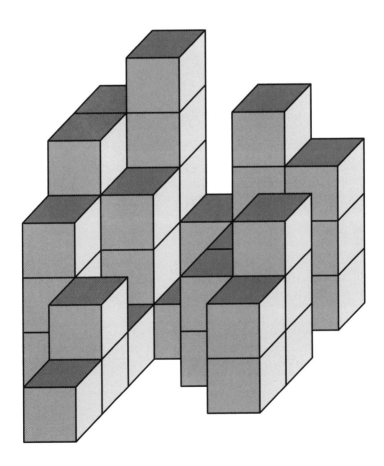

Your solving time: _____

▪ Color by Pixel ▪

Instructions

Color each square according to the key to reveal a hidden picture.

1	1	1	2	2	2	2	2	2	2	2	2	2	2	1	1	1	1	1	2
1	3	4	1	1	2	2	2	2	2	2	2	2	2	1	4	3	1	1	2
1	4	5	5	3	1	2	2	2	1	2	2	2	1	1	5	5	4	1	2
1	3	5	5	5	3	1	1	1	4	1	1	1	3	5	5	5	3	1	2
2	1	3	5	3	3	4	4	4	3	4	4	4	3	3	5	3	1	2	2
2	1	3	3	3	3	3	3	3	4	3	3	3	3	3	3	3	1	2	2
2	2	1	4	3	3	3	3	3	4	3	3	3	3	3	4	1	2	2	2
2	1	4	3	3	3	3	3	3	3	3	3	3	3	4	3	4	1	2	2
2	1	4	3	1	6	1	3	3	3	3	3	1	6	1	3	3	1	2	2
1	4	3	3	1	1	1	3	3	3	3	3	1	1	1	3	4	4	1	2
1	4	4	4	3	3	3	3	7	7	7	3	3	3	3	4	3	4	1	2
1	7	7	4	4	3	3	7	1	1	1	7	3	3	4	4	7	7	1	2
8	1	7	7	7	4	3	7	7	1	7	7	3	4	7	7	7	1	8	9
9	1	7	7	7	7	1	1	7	1	7	1	1	7	7	7	7	1	9	8
8	9	1	1	7	7	7	1	1	1	1	1	7	7	7	7	1	9	8	9
9	8	9	1	1	7	7	7	1	0	1	7	7	7	7	1	1	8	8	9
8	9	8	1	4	1	7	7	7	1	7	7	7	1	1	4	1	9	9	8
9	9	9	1	4	4	1	1	1	1	1	1	1	1	4	4	4	1	9	8
9	8	9	1	1	4	3	4	4	4	4	4	3	4	4	1	9	1	1	1
9	9	8	9	1	4	4	4	3	4	4	4	3	4	4	4	1	1	1	9

1 – black
2 – light blue
3 – orange
4 – brown
5 – dark orange
6 – blue
7 – white
8 – light green
9 – green
0 – pink

Your solving time: _____

▪ **Angular Maze** ▪

Instructions
Find your way through the maze.

Your solving time: _____

▪ **Sequences** ▪

Instructions

Which option, from A to E, should replace the question-mark symbols in order to continue each sequence?

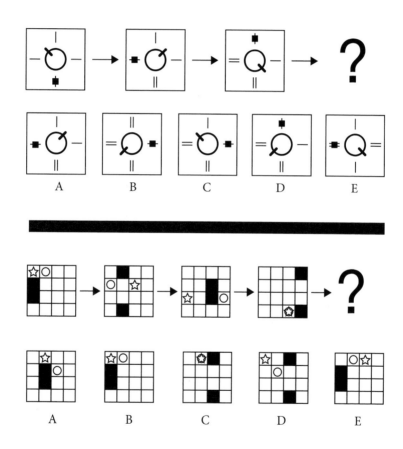

Your solving time: _____

▪ **Building Blocks** ▪

Instructions

Which of the sets of blocks, A to D, can be rearranged to form the assembly shown? All blocks must be used exactly once each.

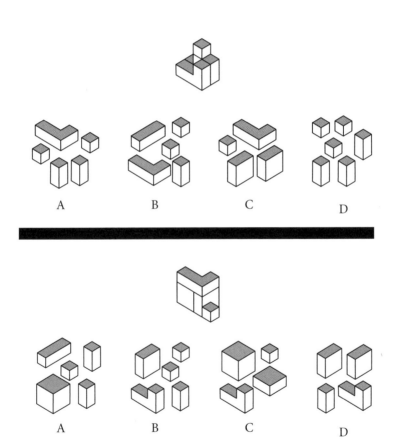

A   B   C   D

A   B   C   D

▪ Missing Face ▪

Instructions

Which of the options, A to E, should replace the blank face on the cube so that they all become different views of the same cube? The correct face may need rotating.

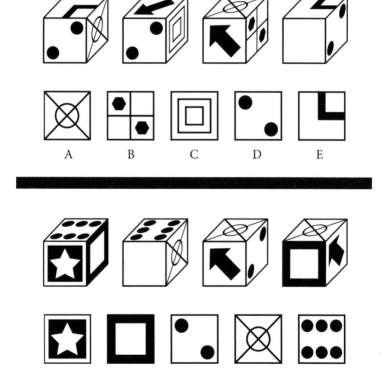

Your solving time: _____

▪ **Upon Rotation** ▪

Instructions
Which of the options, A to E, is exactly the same as the first image of each puzzle, apart from its scale and the angle of its rotation?

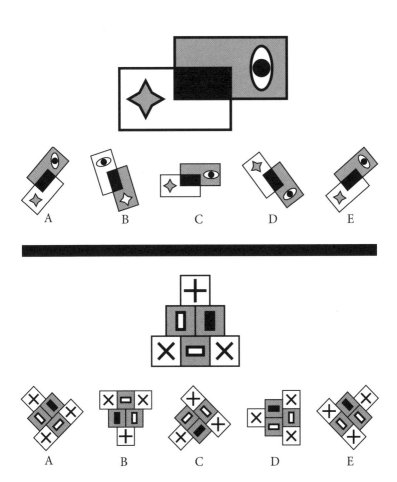

▪ **Color by Shape** ▪

Instructions

Color each shape according to the key to reveal a hidden picture.

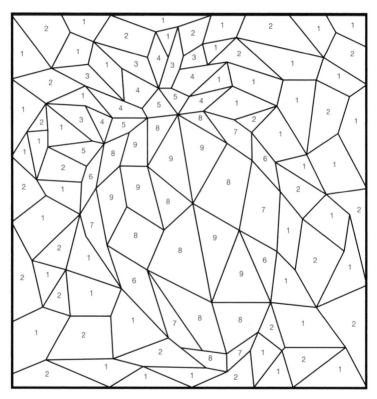

1 – light blue	5 – dark green	9 – dark red
2 – blue	6 – light orange	
3 – light green	7 – orange	
4 – green	8 – red	

Your solving time: _____

▪ Dot to Dot ▪

Instructions

Join the dots with straight lines in increasing numerical order, starting at "1" (marked with a star), to reveal a hidden picture.

Your solving time: _____

▪ **Pattern Poser** ▪

Instructions

Which of the options, A to E, should be placed into the empty box in order to complete the pattern?

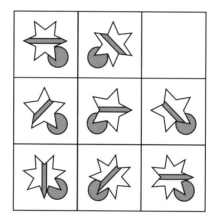

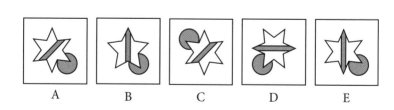

Your solving time: _____

▪ **Wavy Maze** ▪

Instructions
Find your way through the maze.

Your solving time: _____   **119**

▪ **Sequences** ▪

Instructions

Which option, from A to E, should replace the question-mark symbols in order to continue each sequence?

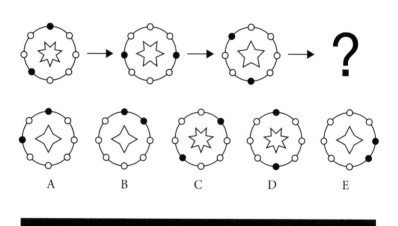

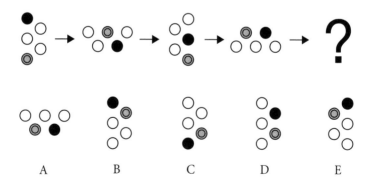

Your solving time: _____

▪ **Find the Rule** ▪

Instructions

Based on the given example transformations, which of the options from A to E should replace the question-mark symbol?

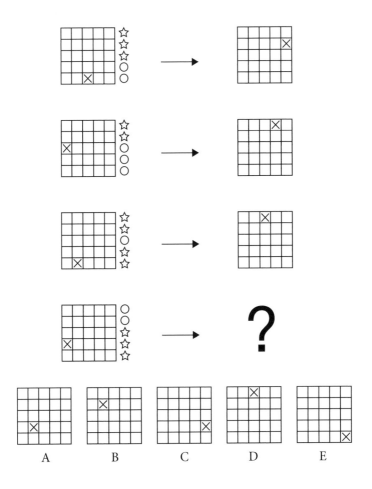

■ Spot the Changes ■

Instructions

Can you find the five differences between the two images?

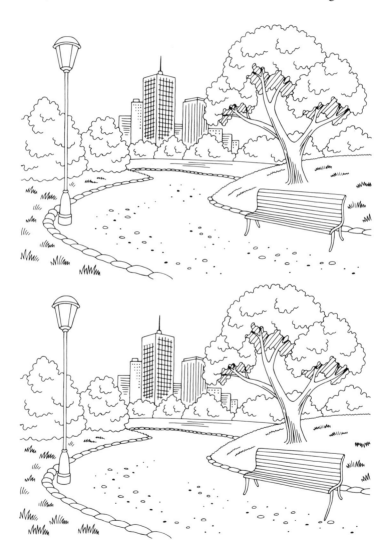

Your solving time: _____

▪ Upon Rotation ▪

Instructions
Which of the options, A to E, is exactly the same as the first image of each puzzle, apart from its scale and the angle of its rotation?

▪ Color by Shape ▪

Instructions

Color each shape according to the key to reveal a hidden picture.

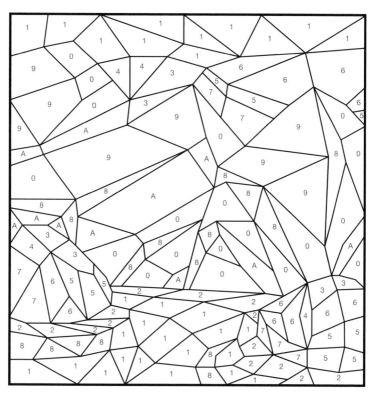

1 – light blue	5 – light brown	9 – light gray
2 – dark blue	6 – brown	0 – gray
3 – light green	7 – dark brown	A – dark gray
4 – green	8 – white	

Your solving time: _____

• Incorrect Cube •

Instructions

If you were to cut out and fold this image to make a six-sided cube, which of the cube images beneath, A to E, could not be formed?

A   B   C   D   E

▪ **Matching Halves** ▪

Instructions
Join the eight halves together to make four complete lion heads.

Your solving time: _____

▪ Dot to Dot ▪

Instructions

Join the dots with straight lines in increasing numerical order, starting at "1"(marked with a star), to reveal a hidden picture.

▪ **Pattern Poser** ▪

Instructions

Which of the options, A to E, should be placed into the empty box in order to complete the pattern?

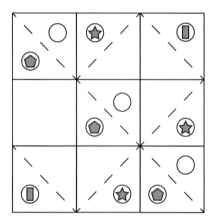

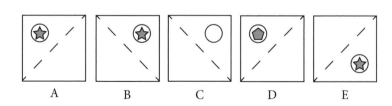

A	B	C	D	E

Your solving time: _____

▪ Rosy Reckoning ▪

Instructions

Which of the images, A to F, exactly matches a portion of the main image?

▪ Transform Again ▪

Instructions

Which option, from A to E, should replace the question-mark symbol? The rule applied on the left of the ":" should also be applied on the right.

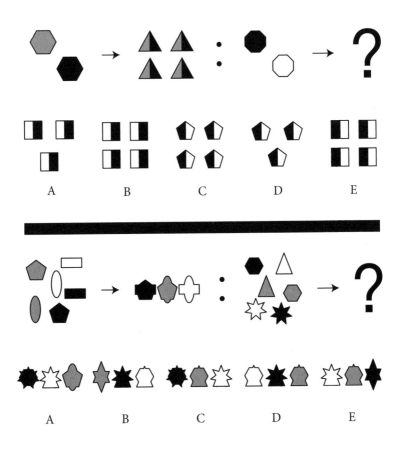

Your solving time: _____

▪ Crack the Code ▪

Instructions

Crack the code used to describe each image, and circle the correct identifier for the image on the second line of each puzzle.

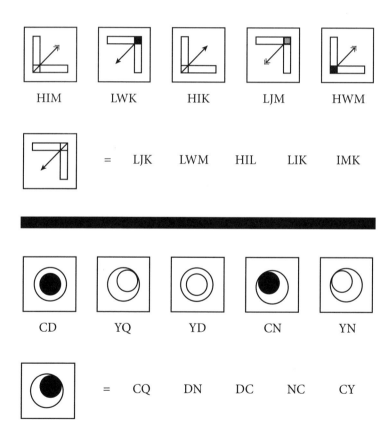

■ **Mirror Image** ■

Instructions

Which of the options, A to E, is an exact mirror image of the lion?

Your solving time: _____

■ **Wavy Maze** ■

Instructions
Find your way through the maze.

▪ Sequences ▪

Instructions

Which option, from A to E, should replace the question-mark symbols in order to continue each sequence?

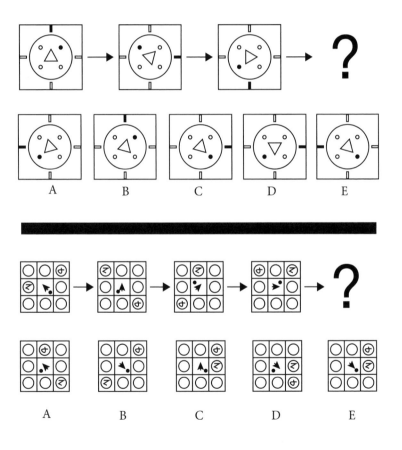

Your solving time: _____

▪ Cubic Conundrum ▪

Instructions

How many cubes are there in the following image? It began as a 5×5×5 block before some cubes were removed. None of the cubes are "floating" in midair.

▪ Color by Pixel ▪

Instructions

Color each square according to the key to reveal a hidden picture.

1	1	1	2	2	3	2	2	2	4	4	4	5	5	4	4	4	2	2	2
1	1	2	2	3	3	2	2	4	6	6	7	4	5	5	5	7	4	2	2
1	2	2	2	2	2	2	2	5	5	6	5	6	6	6	5	5	6	2	2
2	2	2	2	2	2	4	4	7	5	5	6	5	5	5	5	5	5	5	2
2	2	3	3	3	2	4	4	6	6	6	5	5	7	5	8	5	6	7	5
2	3	3	2	2	2	2	6	7	5	8	8	5	5	8	8	5	5	6	6
2	2	2	2	2	2	2	2	2	5	5	8	8	8	8	5	5	7	5	5
2	2	2	2	2	2	2	2	2	2	5	5	8	9	8	2	5	2	2	2
2	2	2	2	3	3	2	3	2	2	2	2	8	9	8	2	2	2	2	2
2	2	2	3	3	2	2	2	2	2	2	8	9	9	8	2	2	2	3	3
2	2	2	2	2	2	2	2	2	2	2	8	9	8	2	2	2	3	3	2
2	2	2	2	2	2	2	2	2	2	2	2	8	8	8	2	2	2	2	2
0	0	0	0	0	0	0	4	4	4	4	4	6	6	6	6	6	6	6	6
6	0	0	3	3	0	0	0	0	4	4	5	6	5	6	6	5	6	5	6
6	5	0	0	0	0	3	0	0	0	0	0	5	5	5	5	6	5	6	6
5	5	8	9	5	0	0	0	3	0	3	0	0	0	0	5	9	9	8	8
5	6	5	5	9	8	9	8	0	0	0	3	0	0	0	0	0	8	9	9
5	5	6	6	5	5	8	8	9	8	0	0	0	0	0	0	3	3	0	0
6	5	6	5	6	5	5	6	5	8	8	8	8	0	0	0	0	0	3	0

1 – yellow   5 – dark green   9 – light brown

2 – light blue   6 – green   0 – blue

3 – light gray   7 – red

4 – light green   8 – brown

Your solving time: _____

▪ Spot the Cube ▪

Instructions

If you were to cut out and fold this image to make a six-sided cube, which of the cube images beneath, A to E, is the only one that could be formed?

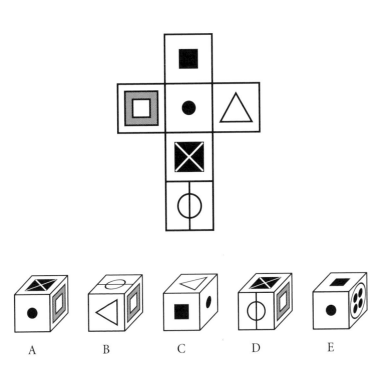

▪ **Find the Pair** ▪

Instructions
Which two of these ballerinas are identical, allowing for rotation?

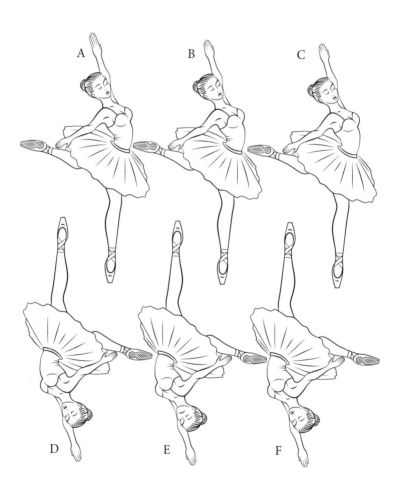

Your solving time: _____

▪ Dot to Dot ▪

Instructions

Join the dots with straight lines in increasing numerical order, starting at "1" (marked with a star), to reveal a hidden picture.

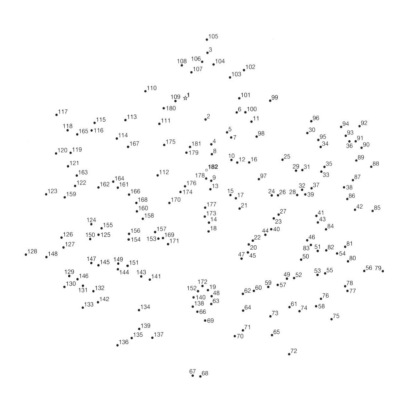

Your solving time: _____

▪ **Pattern Poser** ▪

Instructions

Which of the options, A to E, should be placed into the empty box in order to complete the pattern?

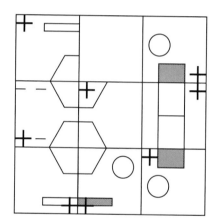

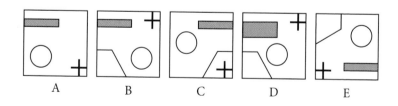

Your solving time: _____

▪ Incorrect Cube ▪

Instructions

If you were to cut out and fold this image to make a six-sided cube, which of the cube images beneath, A to E, could not be formed?

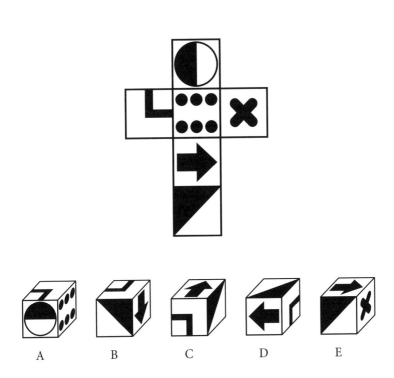

A   B   C   D   E

▪ **Matching Halves** ▪

Instructions

Join the eight halves together to make four complete flowers.

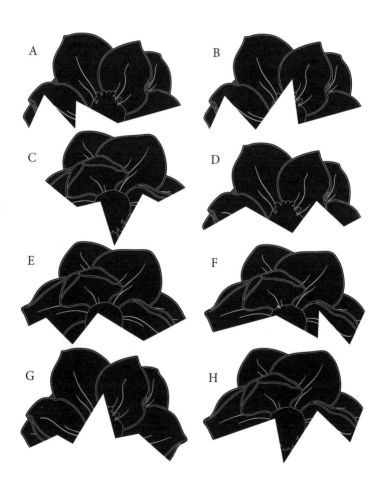

Your solving time: _____

▪ Upon Reflection ▪

Instructions

Which of the options, A to E, would result when each image is reflected in the dashed line shown?

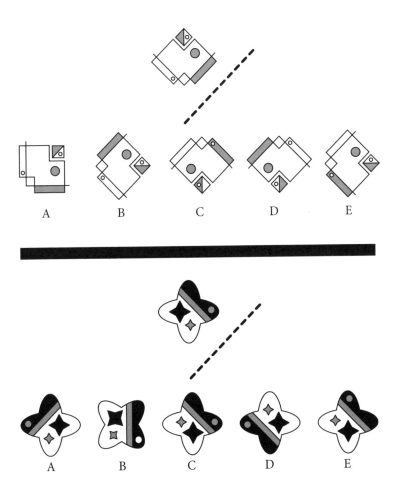

▪ Color by Shape ▪

Instructions

Color each shape according to the key to reveal a hidden picture.

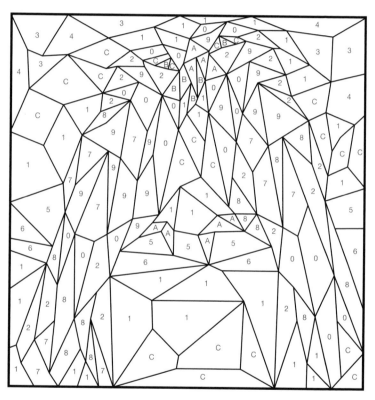

1 – pale blue	5 – light brown	9 – dark orange	C – white
2 – blue	6 – brown	0 – red	
3 – light green	7 – yellow	A – dark gray	
4 – green	8 – orange	B – black	

Your solving time: _____

▪ Find the Rule ▪

Instructions

Based on the given example transformations, which of the options from A to E should replace the question-mark symbol?

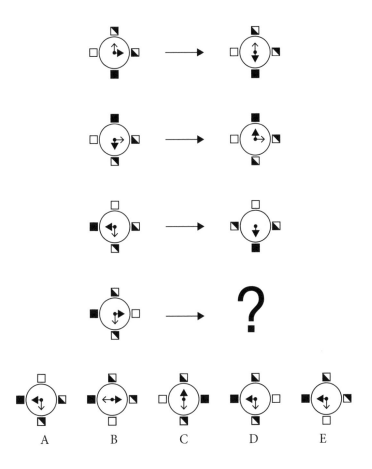

A   B   C   D   E

▪ **What's Changed?** ▪

Instructions
Can you find the five differences between the two images?

Your solving time: _____

▪ Cubic Conundrum ▪

Instructions

How many cubes are there in the following image? It began as a 6×6×6 block before some cubes were removed. None of the cubes are "floating" in midair.

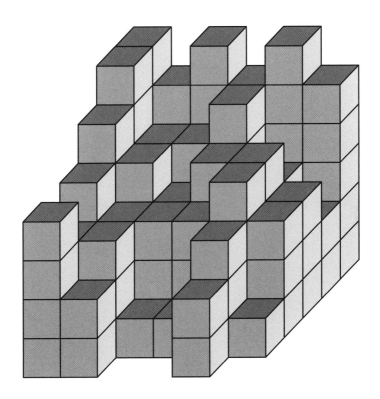

▪ Color by Pixel ▪

Instructions

Color each square according to the key to reveal a hidden picture.

1	1	1	1	1	1	2	2	1	1	1	1	2	2	1	1	1	1	1	2
1	2	1	1	1	1	2	2	2	3	1	1	3	2	3	1	1	1	2	3
2	3	2	4	1	1	2	3	2	2	1	4	2	3	2	1	1	1	3	2
2	3	5	6	4	6	7	3	8	5	4	6	8	3	7	1	4	4	2	8
3	2	2	6	4	6	3	7	3	5	4	6	7	3	5	6	6	4	7	3
3	7	2	6	4	6	7	8	3	3	4	6	3	8	5	6	4	6	7	5
7	5	5	4	6	6	7	7	7	5	4	6	3	7	5	6	6	6	7	7
7	8	3	4	6	6	7	3	8	5	6	6	3	7	7	6	6	6	7	3
7	5	5	4	6	6	7	3	5	5	6	6	7	7	7	6	6	6	7	3
8	5	2	4	6	6	7	3	3	5	6	6	7	5	7	6	4	6	7	5
7	5	7	6	6	6	7	7	3	5	6	6	5	5	7	6	6	6	7	5
7	5	7	6	4	6	7	7	5	7	6	6	5	7	7	4	6	6	7	5
7	7	5	6	4	6	7	5	5	7	6	6	5	7	7	4	6	6	7	5
7	7	5	6	6	6	7	5	5	5	6	6	5	5	7	6	6	6	7	5
7	5	5	6	6	6	7	5	7	5	6	6	5	5	5	6	4	6	7	7
7	5	5	6	4	6	7	5	7	7	6	4	7	7	5	6	4	4	7	4
8	7	7	4	4	6	7	7	7	7	4	4	7	7	4	4	4	4	4	4
7	8	4	4	4	4	7	7	4	4	4	4	4	4	4	4	4	4	1	1
4	4	4	1	1	4	4	4	4	4	4	4	4	1	1	1	1	1	1	1
1	1	1	1	1	1	1	1	1	1	1	1	1	1	1	1	1	1	1	1

1 – light blue   5 – dark green

2 – light green   6 – blue

3 – green   7 – dark gray

4 – white   8 – brown

Your solving time: _____

▪ Dot to Dot ▪

Instructions

Join the dots with straight lines in increasing numerical order, starting at "1" (marked with a star), to reveal a hidden picture.

▪ **Pattern Poser** ▪

Instructions

Which of the options, A to E, should be placed into the empty box in order to complete the pattern?

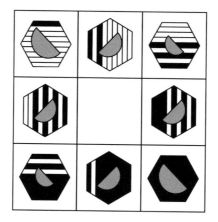

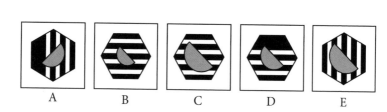

Your solving time: _____

■ **Angular Maze** ■

Instructions
Find your way through the maze.

Your solving time: _____

▪ Sequences ▪

Instructions

Which option, from A to E, should replace the question-mark symbols in order to continue each sequence?

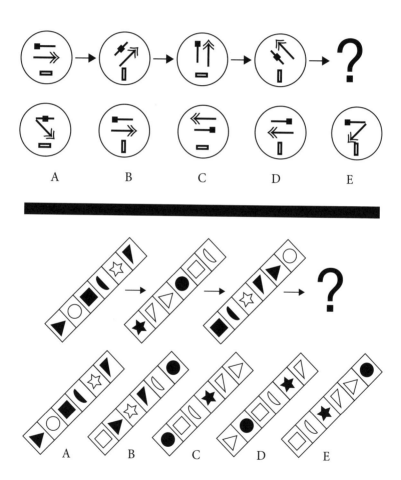

Your solving time: _____

▪ **Shape-Counting** ▪

Instructions

How many triangles, including those formed via overlaps, can you count in this image?

▪ **Pairing Problem** ▪

Instructions
Join these cycling images into identical pairs.

Your solving time: _____

▪ Odd One Out ▪

Instructions
Which image is the odd one out on each line?

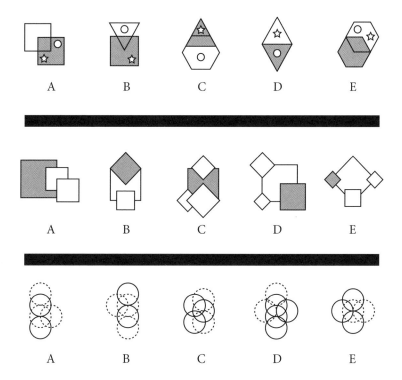

▪ Shape Nets ▪

Instructions

Which of the patterns, A to D, could be cut out and folded to match the view shown at the top?

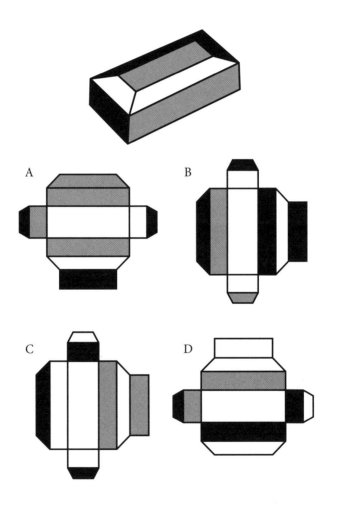

Your solving time: _____

• Cubic Conundrum •

Instructions

How many cubes are there in the following image? It began as a 6×6×6 block before some cubes were removed. None of the cubes are "floating" in midair.

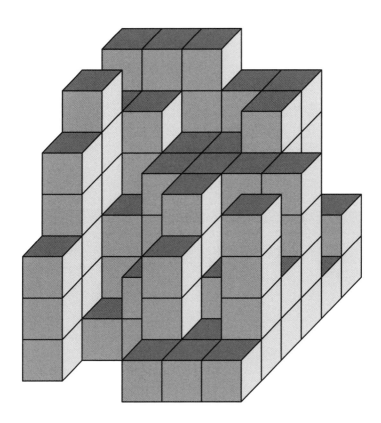

▪ Transform Again ▪

Instructions

Which option, from A to E, should replace the question-mark symbol? The rule applied on the left of the ":" should also be applied on the right.

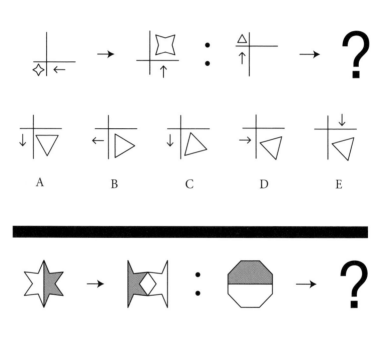

Your solving time: _____

▪ Crack the Code ▪

Instructions

Crack the code used to describe each image and circle the correct identifier for the image on the second line of each puzzle.

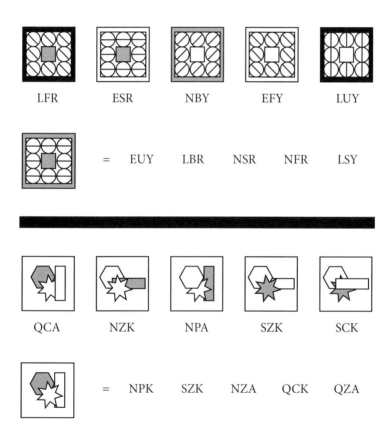

LFR   ESR   NBY   EFY   LUY

=   EUY   LBR   NSR   NFR   LSY

QCA   NZK   NPA   SZK   SCK

=   NPK   SZK   NZA   QCK   QZA

■ **Mirror Image** ■

Instructions

Which of the options, A to E, is an exact mirror image of the eagle?

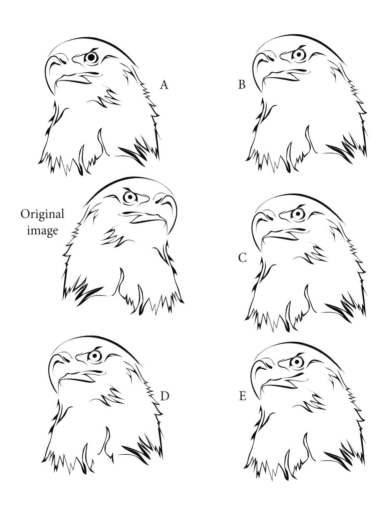

A

B

Original
image

C

D

E

Your solving time: _____

▪ Tracing Paper ▪

Instructions

Which of the options, A to E, represents the view of the image shown at the top when folded in half along the dashed line? Assume it has been drawn on transparent paper.

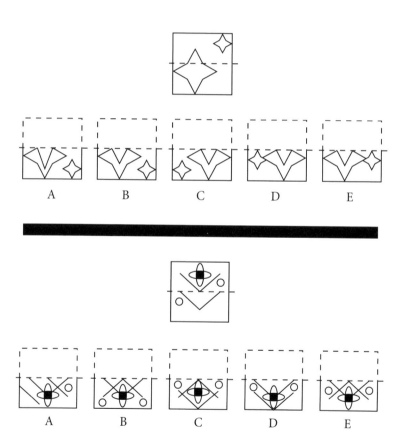

▪ A New View ▪

Instructions

Which of the options, A to D, represents a view of the first 3D object when seen from the direction of the arrow?

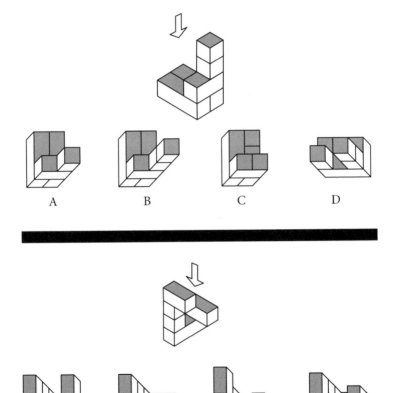

Your solving time: _____

▪ Cubic Conundrum ▪

Instructions

How many cubes are there in the following image? It began as a 6×6×6 block before some cubes were removed. None of the cubes are "floating" in midair.

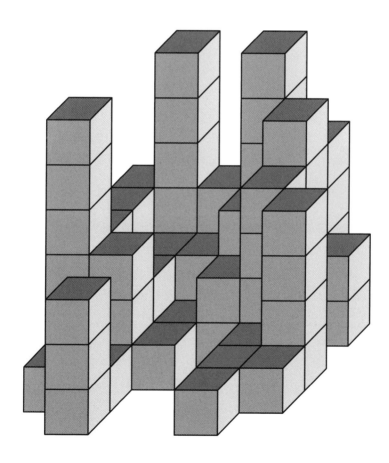

▪ Transform Again ▪

Instructions

Which option, from A to E, should replace the question-mark symbol? The rule applied on the left of the ":" should also be applied on the right.

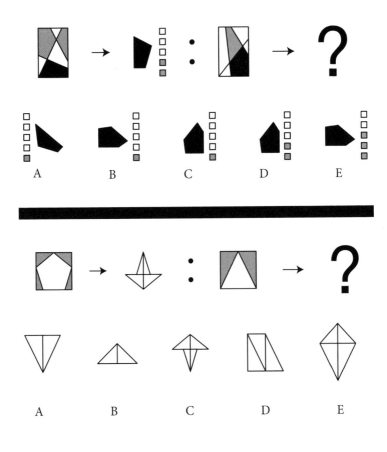

Your solving time: _____

▪ **Pattern Poser** ▪

Instructions

Which of the options, A to D, should be placed into the empty triangle in order to complete the pattern?

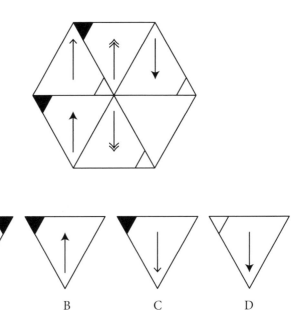

A   B   C   D

▪ A New View ▪

Instructions

Which of the options, A to D, represents a view of the first 3D object when seen from the direction of the arrow?

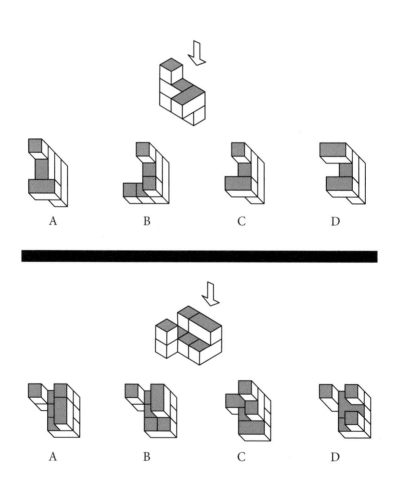

A   B   C   D

A   B   C   D

Your solving time: _____

SOLUTIONS

▪ **Solutions** ▪

Page 7
57 squares and rectangles

Page 8
A-F, B-D, C-E

Page 9
45 cubes

Page 10
Hamburger:

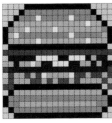

Page 11
B

Page 12
C
A

Page 13
VS – The first letter refers to the color of the rectangles (V = black, P = white). The second letter refers to the orientation of the rectangles (B = horizontal, S = vertical, N = diagonal).
URO – The first letter is the type of shape behind the star (U = circle, A = square, T = pentagon); the second letter is the color of the star (R = gray, M = white); the third letter is the color of the background shape (E = black, O = white).

Page 14
C

Page 15
Sailing boat:

Page 16
D – The stars form a sequence reading from left to right and top to bottom. At each step, the star rotates 45 degrees

▪ Solutions ▪

counterclockwise. The shape in the corner of each square moves around the four corners in a clockwise direction, moving one corner at each step.

Page 17

D – This is the only shape with an arrow pointing at a star rather than away from a star.

A – The other gray bars contain one less circle than the number of corners on their associated polygon.

E – This is the only shape with a clockwise spiral.

Page 18

A

Page 19

C

Page 20

D

B

Page 21

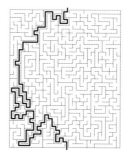

Page 22

A - One point is added to the star and one side is added to the inner polygon at each step.

A - One triangle remains in place, while the second triangle rotates by 45 degrees clockwise at each step using the bottom-left corner of the stationary triangle as the point to rotate around. Each triangle has one circle attached, and each circle moves in a clockwise direction around its triangle, jumping from corner to corner.

Page 23

A – Its top and side faces have been swapped.

▪ Solutions ▪

Page 24
A-C, B-H, D-F, E-G

Page 25
D

Page 26
A
B

Page 27
66 squares and rectangles

Page 28
A-D, B-E, C-F

Page 29
Butterfly:

Page 30
A – The squares form a sequence, reading from left to right and top to bottom. The sequence alternates between reflecting the image vertically and rotating it by 180 degrees, starting with reflection at the first step. When the image is reflected, one gray dot is added. When the image is rotated, one black dot is added.

Page 31
C – This is the only square containing six areas rather than five.
E – This is the only grid containing smaller polygons with a total number of corners that does not equal 15.
C – This is the only image which features a polygon where not all sides are the same length.

Page 32
C

Page 33
UFL – The first letter is the type of white shape (O = star, R = triangle, U = oval); the second letter is the color

▪ **Solutions** ▪

of the square (G = black, E = gray, F = white); the third letter is the location of the square (L = within the shape indicated by letter 1, B = outside of the shape indicated by letter 1).

EJH – The first letter is the orientation of the shape (E = rotated squares above non-rotated squares, N = rotated squares below non-rotated squares, S = rotated squares to the left of non-rotated squares, O = rotated squares to the right of non-rotated squares); the second letter is whether the line going through the rotated squares is dotted or solid (C = dotted, J = solid); the final letter is how many points are on the star (X = 5, H = 6).

Page 34
B

Page 35
E – A has an incorrect top face; B has its front and side faces swapped; C has its top face rotated incorrectly; D has a face that does not appear on the cube net.

Page 36
B and F

Page 37
C
A
D

Page 38
A
D

Page 39
34 cubes

Page 40
The Earth:

▪ **Solutions** ▪

Page 41

D

B

Page 42

A

C

Page 43

B

D

Page 44

Apple tree:

Page 45

A:

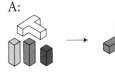

B:

Page 46

E

D

Page 47

A

Page 48

D

E

Page 49

B

C

D

Page 50

B

D

Page 51

C – Each of the left-hand boxes contains one smaller shape which has exactly double the number of sides of another small shape located in the same box. These two shapes snap together in the center of the right-hand box, and the two remaining shapes are shaded black.

173

▪ **Solutions** ▪

Page 52

Page 53

D:

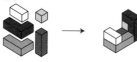

A:

Page 54

B

D

Page 55

C

A

B

Page 56

E

B

Page 57

C

D

Page 58

Mountain landscape:

Page 59

43 squares and rectangles

Page 60

A-F, B-C, D-E

Page 61

A – B has its front and side faces swapped; C has an incorrect side face; D has its front and side faces swapped; E has a face that does not appear on the cube net.

Page 62

C and D

▪ **Solutions** ▪

Page 63
Coat:

Page 64
D – Each row and column has a total of nine white shapes. There are also two shaded shapes in each square, one of which is a circle and the other of which is either a pentagon or a triangle on a checkerboard pattern.

Page 65
B – The number of small squares in the left-hand box matches the number of sides of the outer shape on the right-hand side. If an odd number of small squares in the left-hand box is shaded black, then the central square on the right-hand side will be shaded black; if an even number is shaded black, then the central square on the right-hand side will be white.

Page 66

Page 67
C – Its front and side faces have been swapped.

Page 68
A-H, B-E, C-F, D-G

Page 69

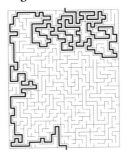

▪ **Solutions** ▪

Page 70

B – The arrow shape within the circle rotates by 180 degrees at each step; the rectangle moves from right to left horizontally across the circle.

A – Shapes remain in the same order, but the empty square moves from right to left by one square per step, while the black shading moves one square right at each step.

Page 71

F

Page 72

D – The colors of the stars have been reversed, and the number of points on each star has been reduced by one. They have been rearranged to sit in a vertical rather than a horizontal line.

B – The three shapes have been spread out into a vertically aligned overlapping set with the largest shape at the top and the smallest at the bottom. The colors of the gray and black shapes have been switched.

Page 73

Crab:

Page 74

C – If you were to rotate each individual grid square by 90 degrees counterclockwise, the solid and dashed lines would join up to make a continuous path running between the boxes. The missing square is the one that would accurately complete this path if it was similarly rotated.

Page 75

A

E

Page 76

B

D

▪ **Solutions** ▪

Page 77
121 squares and rectangles

Page 78
A-D, B-E, C-F

Page 79
B – One dot is removed from the center of the left-hand shape; one side is added to the right-hand shape.

Page 80
The square appears to bend:

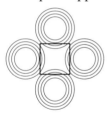

Page 81
56 cubes

Page 82
Flower:

Page 83
B – The undecorated square from the left-hand shape changes color to either black or white, and becomes two small squares at the left and right of the right-hand shape. The two remaining squares overlap in the center of the right-hand shape, with the square featuring an eye design always sitting at the back. The square with an eye shape also rotates by 90 degrees.

Page 84
Surprisingly, the topmost horizontal rectangle matches the vertical rectangle.

▪ Solutions ▪

Page 85
Daisy:

Page 86
E – All of the shapes in the grid squares are a reflection of the shape in the central square, following either vertical, horizontal, or diagonal mirror lines corresponding to the respective shape's position in the grid (for example, the top right square is reflected along a line traveling diagonally from the central-top square to the rightmost square on the central row).

Page 87
A – B has its front face rotated incorrectly; C has an incorrect front face; D has a face that does not appear on the cube net; E has its front and side faces swapped.

Page 88
A and B

Page 89
B:

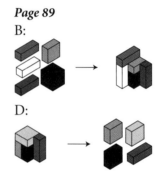

D:

Page 90
D
C

Page 91
D – Each shape is transformed differently: squares are crossed by two perpendicular diagonal lines; black circles are crossed by a horizontal and a vertical line; triangles are bisected by a horizontal or vertical line through their most central

▪ **Solutions** ▪

point. All lines continue to the edge of the grid, except they do not enter squares containing white circles.

Page 92
The bold lines appear to bend, despite being parallel:

Page 93
A – This is the only shape where the number of arrows does not match the number of sides of the polygon.
C – This is the only grid which does not have a row of three shaded squares forming one complete row or column.
B – This is the only image with just one gray shape.

Page 94
D

Page 95
B
C

Page 96
Puppy:

Page 97
A
D
C

Page 98
C
C

Page 99
C
B

▪ Solutions ▪

Page 100
B
A

Page 101
C – The shape which is bisected by a line in the left-hand image becomes a larger shape which surrounds the circle in the right-hand image, and is also filled in black.

Page 102
Both squares are the same size, despite the upper one appearing larger.

Page 103
21 triangles

Page 104
A-F, B-D, C-E

Page 105
B
C

Page 106
A
A

Page 107
Candlestick holder:

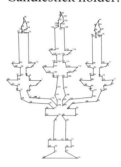

Page 108
B – The small gray ovals are identical in each diagonal line from top left to bottom right, wrapping round the edges of the grid to form three separate diagonals. The remainder of each square forms a sequence, reading from left to right and top to bottom. Two adjacent areas of the large oval change color at each step, working around the circle in a clockwise direction, changing between gray and white. At each step, the central arrow moves to point at the small oval which was shaded gray in the previous step.

▪ **Solutions** ▪

Page 109
42 cubes

Page 110
Fox:

Page 111

Page 112
B – The black square moves clockwise around the outer lines at each step. An extra black line is added in the position where the black square was positioned in the previous step. The line which intersects the circle rotates in a clockwise direction, moving 90 degrees at each step.
B – The two shaded black squares move right by one column at each step, alternating between the central and edge squares. At each step, the star moves down one square and across two squares to the right. The circle moves down one square and across three squares to the right. If any shape would leave the grid, it "wraps around" to the opposite end of the same row or column.

Page 113
A:

C:

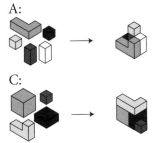

Page 114
C
B

▪ **Solutions** ▪

Page 115
D
B

Page 116
Strawberry:

Page 117
Gecko:

Page 118
E – Reading from left to right and top to bottom, the gray bar rotates 45 degrees clockwise at each step. The stars in the top row have six points, five in the middle row, and seven in the bottom row.

Within each row, the shape in the left-hand column rotates 90 degrees clockwise from the left to the central column, then is reflected vertically from the central to the right column. The gray circle stays in the same horizontal position in each column and vertical position in each row.

Page 119

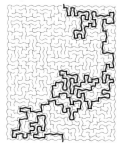

Page 120
A – The number of points on the star decreases by one at each step. The black dot which begins at the top of the circle moves clockwise by two positions around the circle, and the other black dot moves clockwise by one position, at each step.
C – The image rotates

▪ **Solutions** ▪

90 degrees clockwise at each step. The black dot moves diagonally along the arrangement in a zigzag pattern, while the circle with another circle within it moves clockwise around the arrangement.

Page 121
D – Each star to the right of the grid indicates that the cross should travel up one square, while each circle indicates it should travel right one square

Page 122

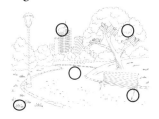

Page 123
E

A

Page 124
Stream between rocks:

Page 125
B – Its front and side faces have been swapped.

Page 126
A-G, B-F, C-D, E-H

Page 127
High heels:

Page 128
A – The circles are in a symmetrical pattern across

▪ **Solutions** ▪

the whole grid, along the diagonal from the top-left to the bottom-right corner. The diagonal dashed lines switch diagonals at each step, reading along the grid squares from left to right and top to bottom. The gray shapes contained within the circles follow a pattern, reading in the same order: pentagon, blank, star, rectangle, star, then repeat.

Page 129
E

Page 130
E – Each shape is split into two identical shapes that together have the same total number of sides. The left of the new shapes is filled with the color of the original left shape and the right with the color of the original right shape.

C – Shapes with matching colors have been combined into a new shape, centering the two shapes together before combining.

Page 131
LIK – The first letter is the orientation of the overall shape (H = corner in bottom left, L = corner in top right); the second letter is the color of the corner square (W = black, I = white, J = gray); the third letter is the type of arrow head (K = solid, M = double lines).

CQ – The first letter is the color of the central circle (C = black, Y = white); the second letter is where the circle is located (D = central, Q = top right, N = top left).

Page 132
A

Page 133

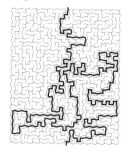

▪ Solutions ▪

Page 134

E – The black dot rotates around the circle in a counterclockwise direction, moving one position at each step. The black rectangle does the same, but moves in a clockwise direction. The central triangle rotates clockwise by 45 degrees at each step.

E – The central arrow rotates clockwise by 45 degrees at each step. The black dot moves between the four corners of the inner square in a clockwise direction. At each step the "z" symbol moves clockwise by one outer circle and the "twist" symbol moves clockwise by two outer circles.

Page 135

35 cubes

Page 136

Tree by river:

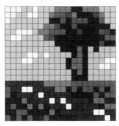

Page 137

A – B has an incorrect side face; C has its top face rotated incorrectly; D has its front and side faces swapped; E has a face that does not appear on the cube net.

Page 138

B and F

Page 139

Maple leaf:

▪ **Solutions** ▪

Page 140

B – Apart from the bold crosses, the entire grid is symmetrical across the horizontal center of the grid. At each step, the cross in the corner of the boxes moves from corner to corner in a clockwise direction, reading from left to right and top to bottom.

Page 141

A – Its front and top faces have been swapped.

Page 142

A-F, B-H, C-G, D-E

Page 143

B

E

Page 144

Parrots on a branch:

Page 145

E – The two arrows in each left-hand shape point to two squares, and these squares switch places in the right-hand shape. The arrow with a solid black head moves to point to the solid black square in the right-hand shape.

Page 146

Page 147

120 cubes

Page 148

Waterfalls:

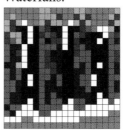

▪ **Solutions** ▪

Page 149

Clownfish:

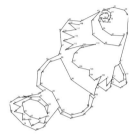

Page 151

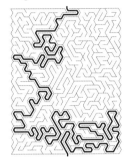

Page 150

C – The squares form a sequence, reading from left to right and top to bottom. The gray semicircle is reflected vertically at each step and changes size in the pattern large, medium, small, medium, large etc. One stripe of the hexagon is shaded black at each step, with alternate stripes being shaded until every other stripe is shaded, after which point the remaining stripes are filled in one at a time. The hexagon rotates by 90 degrees counterclockwise at each step.

Page 152

C – The two lines rotate counterclockwise by 45 degrees at each step. The black square moves to the center of the line after the first step, then to the opposite end of the line, then back to the center, then back to its starting position and so on. The rectangle at the bottom of the circle rotates by 90 degrees at each step.

D – Every shape changes color from either black to white or white to black at each step. The shapes cycle positions, with every shape moving up two boxes at each step, moving into the bottom

187

▪ Solutions ▪

box when they cannot move any further up the grid.

Page 153
27 triangles

Page 154
A-C, B-F, D-E

Page 155
D – This is the only shape made of two non-overlapping shapes (and therefore the only one without two gray areas).
A – This is the only arrangement which does not feature a rotated square.
D – This is the only arrangement made of six circles rather than five.

Page 156
C

Page 157
109 cubes

Page 158
D – The polygon in the smallest area moves to the

largest area and is enlarged plus rotated 45 degrees. The arrow turns to point at the polygon.
B – The two differently shaded pieces swap places.

Page 159
NSR – The first letter is the color of the outlining box (L = black, E = white, N = gray); the second letter is the orientation of the lines in the circles (S = horizontal, U = vertical, F = top left to bottom right, B = top right to bottom left); the final letter is the color of the central box (R = gray, Y = white).
QZA – The first letter defines which shape is shaded gray (Q = hexagon, N = rectangle, S = star); the second letter is which shape is at the front of the arrangement (P = hexagon, C = rectangle, Z = star); the final letter is the orientation of the rectangle (A = vertical, K = horizontal).

Page 160
C

▪ **Solutions** ▪

Page 161
B
E

Page 162
B
D

Page 163
74 cubes

Page 164
B – The black shape has been cut out of the rectangle and rotated clockwise by 90 degrees. The small gray and white squares correspond to the number of gray and white shapes contained within the rectangle, respectively.
A – The gray shapes have been isolated and joined together, then colored white.

Page 165
C – The bottom row of three triangles is the same as the top three triangles if the entire top row was as a whole rotated 180 degrees

and placed beneath itself, and then white triangles became black triangles and vice-versa.

Page 166
C
A

▪ Notes ▪

▪ Notes ▪

■ Notes ■